THE

WELLBEING

GUIDE

- LONDON -

Written & Compiled by
SALLY LOVETT

Photography by
OLIVIA PAYNE

First published in the UK by Vespertine Press 2013

Copyright Vespertine Press 2013
Text copyright Sally Lovett

Photography copyright Olivia Payne.
Other images courtesy of:
p.33 & p.149 - Como Shambhala; p.115, bottom - Hot Bikram;
p.129 - Tooting Bec Lido, p.45 - Down To Earth Café; p.47, top - Triyoga;
p.49-51 - Evolve Wellness Centre

A catalogue of this book is available from the British Library

ISBN 978-0-9566582-4-1

Design by Matt Barker - artwerk.co.uk
Covers by James Kirkup - james-kirkup.co.uk
Digital mapping by Encompass Graphics Ltd, Hove, UK
encompass-graphics.co.uk

Printed and bound in the UK by Four Corners Print
This book has been printed on paper produced by sustainably managed forests.

Set in TR Avalon, **U.S. 101** & Raleway

Also available from Vespertine Press -
The Independent Coffee Book London & *Craft Beer London*

vespertinepress.co.uk

CONTENTS

NORTH

SOUTH

WORDS OF WELLBEING

USING THIS GUIDE

The first part of this book serves as a guide to the best wellbeing places in London. They're divided into five key areas comprising Central, North, South, East and West, so you can find places depending on your location. The wellbeing places are categorised further still into:

Eat: Healthy eateries serving vegetarian, vegan, raw or organic food.

Relax: Calm-inducing places to find peace and serenity.

Move: Places to activate endorphins with heart-rate raising pursuits.

Each feature includes key information about the wellbeing place, including opening hours and the nearest train stations and bus stops. (Please note bus information only denotes services to the nearest stop. Alternative routes may also be available) We've avoided including places with hefty membership fees, so anywhere included in this guide can be enjoyed and visited on a casual drop-in basis.

The second part of this book is 'Words of Wellbeing' comprising expert advice and information from some of London's leading wellbeing practitioners to inspire and inform your pursuit of a healthier lifestyle. Finally, at the back of the book you'll find maps to help you find all the places featured in the guide

FOREWORD
BY
TESSA WATT

London - A metropolitan area of over 12 million people, a history of 2,000 years and with more than 300 languages spoken. It's enormous, rambling, creative, frenetic, infuriating, chaotic and inspiring.

We Londoners have a love-hate relationship with this city. Its adrenalin courses through our veins like the map of the Underground. Sometimes the pace of city life speeds us up and drives us to distraction. We stand on the platform cursing our three minute wait for the next train, staring at a billboard which promises us a turquoise sea and a far-away beach.

But then we remember - that peace and wellbeing are not just for the holidays; not something to put off for some other time or place. Increasingly, we Londoners are discovering that we can find our health and happiness right here, right now, in the midst of our big crazy city.

This guidebook is a testament to an increasing prioritisation of wellbeing amongst Londoners. Carry it with you, and it will remind you of three things you can do for yourself every day: eat well, exercise and relax. Which do you need right now? Is it time for a lunch break and a chat with a friend? Do you need to get moving, raise your heart rate and stretch? Or is it time to stop doing and sit for a while, just being? If we can slow down and listen, our own bodies and hearts will tell us what we need.

Wherever you are in the city, somewhere not far away, you can find healthy, inspiring food. What a change from when I first moved here in the late 1980s, when typical café fare was a greasy fry-up. Now the restaurants in this book offer a stunning range of vegetarian, vegan, raw and organic menus, bringing creativity and care into the whole process, from sourcing to cooking to eating.

All over London, you can find unusual, surprising ways to move the body and keep fit, from wall-climbing to boxing to street jazz . And in almost every neighbourhood now you'll find a yoga or meditation centre. A few decades ago, sitting in silence was considered new-age and left-field. Now meditation classes are packed with professionals, students, doctors, accountants, taxi drivers - people from every walk of life.

Within even the busiest day, we can make time for mindfulness. We can slow down when eating, to really taste our food. We can make time for stillness, and also time for movement. We can decide that rather than rushing through our lives and our city, we will make a choice to appreciate the present moment.

TESSA WATT
Slow Down London   www.slowdownlondon.co.uk
Being Mindful   www.beingmindful.co.uk

CENTRAL

42°RAW

6 Burlington Gardens W1S 3EX
Tel: 020 7300 8059

Online	www.42raw.co.uk
Hours	Mon-Sat: 8.30am-6pm
Average price	£7 for a main meal
Trains	Piccadilly Circus / Green Park
Buses	14, 22 - Royal Academy or 15, 159, 453, 6, 13 - Conduit Street

CENTRAL

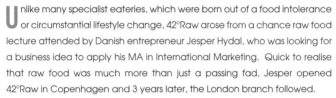

WELLBEING EAT

Unlike many specialist eateries, which were born out of a food intolerance or circumstantial lifestyle change, 42°Raw arose from a chance raw food lecture attended by Danish entrepreneur Jesper Hydal, who was looking for a business idea to apply his MA in International Marketing. Quick to realise that raw food was much more than just a passing fad, Jesper opened 42°Raw in Copenhagen and 3 years later, the London branch followed.

Based at the back of the Royal Academy, 42°Raw isn't your average museum café. Raw lasagne, Thai noodles and tapas are lunchtime favourites; chia-cocoa pudding with banana and hemp seeds are a breakfast classic; and the green juices, smoothies, brownies, cakes and cookies keep the local Mayfair masses working, shopping - and in the case of the topless male models in the clothes shop across the road - posing throughout the day. Based on the belief that food should be served in its most natural state, 42°Raw uses only 100% plant-based foods, all untouched by sugar, dairy, preservatives and colouring to create a menu of meals, snacks, treats and drinks that simply scream health, vitality… and instagram-worthy food photos.

The neutral décor of the restaurant – which is a merger of organic farmer's market meets modern Mayfair – provides a modest backdrop to showcase the mouth-watering colours and textures on offer. Despite being raw in name, 42°Raw is 'plant-based' in nature, serving 100% plant-based food, rather than a menu that adheres to the strict definition of raw (unprocessed vegan foods that have not been heated above 46°C).

This decision to deviate from the 'raw' definition of their name was born from the experience of two chilly Copenhagen winters, when warming soups and risottos were called for on their menu. Not unfamiliar with a biting cold climate, London's 42°Raw will be following suit and adding vegetable soups and brown rice risotto with white truffle oil and oyster mushrooms to their menu during autumn and winter.

Slightly limited by a 6pm close time, which is dictated by the Royal Academy opening hours, 42°Raw misses out on the opportunity to serve a leisurely evening meal, but all items are displayed pre-packaged in the fridge and ready to be taken away and enjoyed for dinner elsewhere. For those dining during the day, however, it's worthwhile eating in the indoor seating to absorb the museum ambience, or people watch the goings-on of W1 from the outdoor tables and chairs.

Using an understated, rather than a smug and evangelical approach to healthy living, 42°Raw is working hard to develop a mainstream following and appeal that transcends the raw foodist community alone. With it's superb central location, affable staff, delicious dishes and affordable prices, the future of 42°Raw looks radiantly healthy.

TITBITS

12-14 Heddon Street W1B 4DA
Tel: 020 7758 4110

Online	www.titbits.co.uk @titbits_uk
Hours	Mon-Weds: 9am-10:30pm Thurs-Sat: 9am-12am Sun: 11:30am-10:30pm
Average price	£8-10 for a main meal
Trains	Piccadilly Circus / Oxford Circus
Buses	C2, 6, 12, 28, 159, 453 - Conduit Street

WELLBEING EAT

Referring to themselves as a fast food restaurant due to their self-serve 'weigh and pay' system (with most platefuls weighing in at a reasonable £8-£10), Swiss-born titbits turns fast food's bad press on it's head with a 'buffet boat' of colourful, seasonal and GM-free vegetarian food that will entice even the most dedicated carnivore to give a meat-free meal a chance. The buffet menu changes on a seasonal basis and blends European dishes such as tofu goulash stroganoff with exotic meals from further afield, like chickpea pubjabi chole. Salads, snacks, appetizers and desserts also feature heavily and provide even more excuses to return to the buffet boat for a second helping.

Unlike other fast food restaurants, your time at titbits can be a leisurely affair, and the stylish décor, extensive drinks menu and comfy seating encourage most diners to make an afternoon or evening out of their visit. Having built up a loyal customer following since opening in 2008, titbits' sheer popularity, positive press and central London location is proving the place of vegetarianism in mainstream cuisine.

WHOLE FOODS MARKET

20 Glass House Street, Piccadilly W1B 5AR
Tel: 020 7406 3100

Online	www.wholefoodsmarket.com /stores/piccadilly @wfm_piccadilly
Hours	Mon-Fri: 7.30am-9.30pm Sat: 9am-9.30pm Sun: 11am-9pm
Average price	£7 for a small salad from the salad bar
Trains	Piccadilly Circus
Buses	453 - Portland Place or 18, C2 - New Cavendish Street

CENTRAL

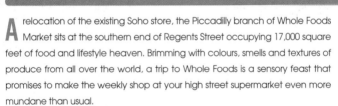

A relocation of the existing Soho store, the Piccadilly branch of Whole Foods Market sits at the southern end of Regents Street occupying 17,000 square feet of food and lifestyle heaven. Brimming with colours, smells and textures of produce from all over the world, a trip to Whole Foods is a sensory feast that promises to make the weekly shop at your high street supermarket even more mundane than usual.

As well as aisle upon aisle of natural and organic produce, there's a juice and smoothie bar, patisserie, cupcake, cheese and pizza counters, a 'Greens, Grains and Beans' salad bar, a bakery, florist, charcuterie, a beauty department devoted to natural skincare, and upstairs seating with free wifi and weekly in-store tastings and cooking demonstrations. But compulsive shoppers and impulse buyers be warned – affectionately nicknamed 'Whole Paycheck', Whole Foods customers on a budget might want to opt for a basket over a shopping trolley, or at least make a beeline for the more moderately priced '365 value' range.

Whether it's grinding your own peanut butter from scratch at the peanut butter station, finally tracking down an elusive ingredient you've been searching for for months, or tucking into the free samples handed out by staff with mega watt smiles, Whole Foods turns an errand into an experience, making it almost impossible to simply nip in for one item without at least a browse. For customers so impressed by their shopping experience, there are branded t-shirts, hats and water bottles to pledge true allegiance to the Whole Foods lifestyle.

Although occasionally criticised for the excessive air miles that stocking such an array of international produce inevitably entails, Whole Foods attempt to strike a balance by also stocking various local and much loved London brands, such as Borough's Monmouth coffee, speciality breads from Clerkenwell's St John's Bakery and soya, vegan and gluten free cupcakes from Battersea's Cat & the Cream bakery. This commitment to trading with local suppliers adds weight to the company mission to support local communities, an endeavor which is supported further by their '5% day' initiative, whereby stores donate 5% of the day's profits to a local charity several times a year.

Whole Foods entered the UK market in 2007 with a 3 storey, 80,000 square foot store on Kensington High Street, with further stores in Clapham, Stoke Newington, Camden and this Piccadilly branch having opened since. With plans to open stores in Fulham and Richmond later in the year, it seems Londoners are loving the Whole Foods American dream, proving further still the increasing priority of wellbeing on our personal agendas and pockets.

DISCOVER EARTH'S FINEST WATER.

Whether you practice Pilates, yoga, or dance, FIJI Water is the perfect choice to replenish and recover from your workout. Rich in naturally occurring minerals and electrolytes, FIJI Water delivers hydration with uncompromised taste.

Sipping water all day need not be dull or bland. With FIJI Water, you'll discover natural hydration with an unmistakable silky quality and refreshing taste. It is FIJI's unique blend of minerals that combine perfectly to create that soft, smooth mouthfeel and signature taste that you'll enjoy with each sip. (At least, that's how the world's sommeliers and top chefs describe us; you decide).

What connoisseurs of all things natural and nurturing need to know is that our water comes from a pristine, one of a kind source. Located on the edge of a tropical rainforest, FIJI Water collects in an artesian aquifer while filtering through layers of volcanic rock and clay, becoming rich in earth's natural minerals. Bottled via a sealed system, it remains protected and untouched until you open the cap. Discover the perfect water to complement your lifestyle. However and whenever you draw nourishment in your life.

Choose from FIJI's 1L, 500mL and 330mL bottles, perfect for active lifestyles. You can find FIJI Water at the likes of Whole Foods Markets, Alchemy Yoga Centre in Camden and other discerning retailers.

- Artesian water from a pristine source
- Untouched, until you unscrew the cap
- Unique soft flavour and silky-smooth mouth-feel
- Hydration helps keeps body and mind in balance

WILD FOOD CAFÉ

1st floor, 14 Neal's Yard, Covent Garden WC2H 9DP
Tel: 020 7419 2014

Online	www.wildfoodcafe.com @WildFoodCafe
Hours	Sun-Weds: 12-5pm Thurs-Sat: 12-10pm
Average price	£9 for a main course
Trains	Covent Garden / Leicester Square
Buses	8, 29, 55, 134, 242 - Tottenham Court Road station

WELLBEING
EAT

Another of London's wellbeing hubs, Neal's Yard is a hidden square situated off Neal Street, offering some respite from the hustle of neighbouring Covent Garden. Wild Food Café is Neal's Yard's new kid on the block, having opened a raw-centric vegetarian and vegan café in November 2011 and an accompanying smoothie bar – 'The Wild Juicery' - a year later.

Comprising an open plan kitchen surrounded by bar stool seating, three large communal tables and bedecked with fluttering Himalayan prayer flags, Wild Food Café bursts with colour and flavour and is abuzz with enthusiastic and passionate staff.

The menu is packed with 'sunfoods' served below 39°c, superfoods, freshly foraged wild foods and locally sourced organic goods. The 'Forgotten Ecstasy' smoothie, made with chocolate freshly ground on site, is divine and the in-house vegan burger claims to be the meatiest vegan burger in town. And with rumours circulating that the biodynamic wine on the menu is hangover-free, Neal's Yard looks set to be busier than ever.

INDABA

18 Hayes Place, Marylebone NW1 6UA
Tel: 020 7724 9994

Online	www.indabayoga.com
	@indabayoga
Hours	Mon-Fri: 6.30am-9.15pm
	Sat & Sun: 9am-6:30pm
Average class price	£13 for a 60 min class
Trains	Baker Street / Edgware Road / Marylebone
Buses	13,18,139,205, 453 - Lisson Grove

WELLBEING RELAX

Meaning 'gathering', Indaba opened it's doors in 2011 to a yoga space bedecked with rich dark wooden flooring, aubergine coloured walls and red cushions which immediately create a warm earthy hue that welcomes all who walk through its doors. Complimentary herbal tea adds to the homely feel of the studio, whilst the top notch changing facilities add a splash of Marylebone chic.

Keen to offer a diversity of styles suitable for yoga practitioners of all abilities, Indaba's timetable balances beginner's courses with Dharma Mittra masterclasses, and every style in between, all taught by some of London's most esteemed teachers. Classes take place in two spacious studios, using red yoga mats and props - which make a welcome change to the purple colour scheme that many London yoga studios rigorously adopt. Away from Indaba, be sure to befriend them on Facebook for yoga chat to tide you over until you're next on the mat and for daily inspiration to encourage you to come back for more.

THE SCHOOL OF LIFE

70 Marchmont Street WC1N 1AB
Tel: 020 7833 1010

Online	www.theschooloflife.com
	@theschooloflife
Hours	Shop: Mon- Fri: 12-6pm. Open evenings and weekends for specific events
Average price	£30 for a 3 hour seminar
Trains	Russell Square / Euston / Kings Cross
Buses	59, 68, 91,168, 188 - Tavistock Square

WELLBEING
RELAX

A somewhat anomalous entry in the 'relax' category, but a credible contribution to London's wellbeing nonetheless, The School of Life runs programmes and services offering ideas and inspiration to live wisely and well. With a faculty that reads like a 'who's who' of modern day philosophers, cultural thinkers and creatives, The School of Life is adeptly equipped to tackle the important questions, topics and conundrums of every day life.

Founded in 2008 by philosopher Alain de Botton and former Tate Modern curator Sophie Howarth, The School of Life is a shop, classroom and consultation room based in Bloomsbury - an appealing area that's aptly rife with academia, rich in culture and history and conveniently close to Kings Cross for their increasing number of European visitors.

The School of Life's classes, workshops, courses and 'Sunday sermons' take place predominantly on evenings and weekends (bar the five day intensives during the week) and attract a following of curious and hungry minds. The programme of events is eclectic and responsive to the dilemmas of the School's clientele with popular classes including 'How to find a job you love', 'How to have better conversations', and 'How to treat your nature deficit.' There are also courses and sermons on sex, boredom, violence, humanity and plenty of other meaty topics, as well as walking tours, weekend retreats and week-long intensives - all of which are taught and presented by celebrated and renowned experts in these respective fields.

Beyond their classroom, The School of Life has earned international acclaim from tours of Sydney, Amsterdam, New York and Rio, as well as stints on the UK festival circuit closer to home.

Back in Bloomsbury, The School of Life's new 'Couch' service offers one-off 'personal MOT' consultations, which intend to offer stigma-free, high street therapy, that's regarded with the same necessity and social acceptance as a visit to the hairdresser or dentist. The MOTs cover life, career, relationships and creativity, and are led by expert therapists affiliated with The School of Life.

Also taking place in the therapy room is the bibliotherapy service: a consultation, followed by bespoke recommendations of books to enchant, enrich and inspire. The School of Life's series of self-help books - which examine work, sex, money, maturity and changing the world - no doubt features in the bibliotherapy consultations, alongside other thought-provoking titles that can be found in The School of Life's brilliant shop on the ground floor.

Appealing to a generation and social shift that prioritises personal fulfillment over more superficial measures of self-worth and wealth, the School of Life is an enterprising concept that will challenge and inspire even the most tired of minds to reap the very most out of every day.

COMO SHAMBHALA

The Metropolitan Hotel, Old Park Lane W1K 1LB
Tel: 020 7447 5750

CENTRAL

Online	www.comohotels.com/metropolitanlondon/wellbeing @COMOhotels
Hours	Mon-Sun: 9am-9pm
Average price	£90 for a 60 min treatment
Trains	Hyde Park Corner
Buses	2, 16, 36 - London Hilton Hotel

WELLBEING
RELAX

A holistic spa offering Asian inspired therapies, the Como Shambhala Urban Escape Spa is housed within the Metropolitan hotel, and welcomes members of the public as well as hotel guests.

The somewhat chaotic location of Hyde Park Corner may not be as serene a location as the sister spas in Bali, Thailand and the Maldives, but once inside Como Shambhala's London branch, wrapped in a fluffy white robe and sipping their signature blend of ginger tea (which those who have been to spas in the Far East will fondly recognise as the traditional pre or post-treatment replenishment) you might find you stop hankering to be in the Maldives after all.

Derived from the Buddhist term 'Shambhala', meaning 'sacred place of bliss', the spa strives to create exactly that with a menu of massage, facials and beauty treatments to soothe body, mind and spirit.

The products used in the treatments are Como Shambhala's own brand - rich in essential oils, free from anything artificial and available to buy in the in-spa shop following your treatment.

MILDREDS VEGETARIAN RESTAURANT

45 Lexington Street W1F 9AN
www.mildreds.co.uk
Hours: Mon-Sat: 12pm-11pm
Trains: Oxford Circus / Piccadilly Circus Tube
Buses: 6, 13, 23, 139 - Conduit Street / Hamleys

VITAO

74 Wardour Street W1F 0TE
www.vitao.co.uk
Hours: Mon-Sat: 12-11pm, Sun: 12-9pm
Trains: Tottenham Court Road Tube
Buses: 14, 19, 38 - Dean Street / Chinatown
or 24, 136 Cambridge Circus

YOTOPIA

www.yotopia.co.uk
13 Mercer Street, WC2H 9QJ
Hours: Mon: 12-8.30pm, Tues-Fri: 7.15am-8.45pm
Sat: 10.30am-3pm, Sun: 11,30am-1pm & 6-7pm
(or check online for class times)
Trains: Leicester Square / Covent Garden Tube
Buses: 14, 19, 24, 29, 38, 176 - Cambridge Circus

VANILLA BLACK

17 Took's Court EC4A 1LB
www.vanillablack.co.uk
Hours: Mon-Fri: 12-2.30pm and 6-10pm, Sat: 6-10pm
Trains: Chancery Lane Tube
Buses: 8, 242 - Chancery Lane Tube

PLANET ORGANIC

22 Torrington Place WC1E 7HJ
www.planetorganic.com
Hours: Mon-Fri: 7.30am-9pm, Sat: 9am-8pm,
Sun: 12-6pm
Trains: Goodge Street Tube
Buses: 10, 14, 24, 29, 73 - Goodge Street Tube

THE LIGHT CENTRE

www.lightcentrebelgravia.co.uk
7-9 Eccleston Street SW1W 9LX
Hours: Mon-Fri: 7am-9.30pm, Sat: 8am-4pm
(or check online for class times)
Trains: London Victoria Rail & Tube
Buses: C10, 11, 170, 211 - Eccleston Bridge

INNER SPACE

36 Shorts Gardens WC2H 9AB
www.innerspace.org.uk
Hours: Mon-Sat: 10.30am-6pm
Trains: Tottenham Court Road / Covent Garden Tube
Buses: 8, 29, 55, 134, 242 - Tottenham Court Road Tube

COLLEGE OF NATUROPATHIC MEDICINE

41 Riding House Street W1W 7BE
www.naturopathy-uk.com
Hours: Mon-Sat: Check online for class times
Trains: Goodge Street Tube
Buses: C2, 88, 453 - New Cavendish Street

THE PLACE

17 Duke's Road WC1H 9PY
www.theplace.org.uk
Hours: Mon-Sun: Check online for class times
Trains: Euston Tube
Buses: 59, 68, 91, 168 - Upper Woburn Place

PINEAPPLE DANCE STUDIOS

7 Langley Street WC2H 9JA
www.pineapple.uk.com
Hours: Mon-Fri: 10.30am-9.30pm, Sat: 10am-6.30pm, Sun: 12-5.30pm
Trains: Leicester Square / Covent Garden Tube
Buses: 14, 19, 24, 29, 38, 176 - Cambridge Circus

H2 BIKE TO RUN

Dufours Place (just off Broadwick St.) W1F 7SP
www.h2bikerun.co.uk
Hours: Mon-Fri: 6am-9.30pm, Sat: 10am-4pm
Trains: Oxford Circus Tube
Buses: 7, 8, 10, 25, 73, 390 - Wardour Street

OASIS SPORTS CENTRE

32 Endell Street WC2H 9AG
www.better.org.uk/leisure/oasis-sports-centre/
Hours: Mon-Fri: 6.30am-10pm, Sat: 9.30am-6pm
Sun: 9.30am-6pm
Trains: Tottenham Court Road Tube
Buses: 8, 29, 55, 134, 242, 390 - Tottenham Court
Road Tube

SERPENTINE RUNNING CLUB

Seymour Place W1H 5TH
www.serpentine.org.uk
Hours: Training sessions Mon-Sun. Check online for
class times
Trains: Edgware Road Tube
Buses: 6, 7, 16, 23, 39, 98, 419 - Sussex Gardens

RAPHA CYCLING CLUB

85 Brewer Street W1F 9ZN
www.rapha.cc
Hours: Thursday evening rides depart at 6.30pm.
Check online for details of weekend rides.
Trains: Piccadilly Circus Tube
Buses: 3, 12, 15, 88, 94, 159 - Piccadilly Circus Tube

LONDON FRIDAY NIGHT SKATE & SUNDAY STROLL ROLLERBLADING

Routes vary around central London
www.lfns.co.uk
Hours: Fridays 8-10pm, Sundays 2-4pm

WEST

DAYLESFORD FARM SHOP & CAFÉ

208-212 Westbourne Grove, Notting Hill W11 2RH
Tel: 020 7313 8050

WEST

Online	www.daylesfordorganic.com @daylesfordfarm
Hours	Mon - Sat: 8am-7pm Sun: 10am-4pm
Average price	£10 for a main course
Trains	Notting Hill Gate
Buses	28, 31, 328 - Pembridge Villas or 7, 23, 70 - Cheapstow Road

WELLBEING
EAT

Amongst the boutiques, avant garde florists and designer shops of affluent Westbourne Grove, Daylesford Farm Shop and Café feeds West Londoner's wellbeing with a wholesome offering of sustainably farmed, organic produce. Farming organically for the past 25 years, Daylesford employ a 'from farm to fork' modus operandi, stocking their café, shop, bakery, butchers and creamery with daily deliveries of fresh and seasonal produce direct from their Gloucester farm.

Spread over three levels, impeccably styled to resemble a bygone era of rustic farm shops, Daylesford's Notting Hill branch accommodates diners and shoppers alike, with in-house and pavement seating for eating, and shelf upon shelf of own-brand produce, homeware and lifestyle items to recreate the Daylesford experience at home.

Busy throughout the day, the café is a particularly popular spot for weekend brunch, where runny eggs benedict is best served on the pavement terrace whilst watching the beautiful Notting Hill set sashay past. Salads, freshly baked breads, home-reared meats and artisan cheeses feature on the lunch menu, whilst cakes such as the organic Manuka honey, almond and lemon drizzle will tempt many for afternoon tea. The farm shop stocks everything from chutnies to ready-made chicken casserole, mostly packaged responsibly in Daylesford's signature, understated style.

The Notting Hill branch is Daylesford's second London site, with a similar sized farm shop and café in Pimlico and a concession in Selfridge's food hall. Daylesford's flagship farm shop is on the farm itself, which sits in 2,000 acres of Cotswolds countryside, alongside a café, cookery school and their 'Hay Barn Spa.' Offering indulgent treatments and yoga, Pilates and meditation classes, the Hay Barn Spa hosts drop-in visitors during the day, or guests staying for an immersive weekend retreat.

Although the first Daylesford farm shop opened in Gloucester in 2002, their farm was founded ten years years prior by Carole Bamford, a young mother and advocate for the organic farming movement. Twenty one years on, with Carole still at the helm as Creative Director, Daylesford has amassed an impressive harvest of hundreds of varieties of fruit and vegetables and thriving livestock for their animal products. One of the most sustainable farms in the UK, Daylesford pride themselves on farming organically, sourcing locally, packaging lightly and protecting natural resources. Their ecological efforts are clearly paying off, as they've won over 120 awards to date, including UK's Best Organic Retailer.

For Londoners who crave a more sustainable, organic and environmentally responsible way of life, but struggle with the limitations and practicalities of living in a city, Daylesford provides the menu and the means to the lifestyle they desire – without having to get a speck of mud on their wellies.

DOWN TO EARTH CAFÉ

240 Kensington High Street W8 6ND
Tel: 020 7371 6987

WEST

Online	www.downtoearth.co.uk @downtoearthken
Hours	Mon-Sun: 7.30am-10.30pm
Average price	£8 for a main course
Trains	Kensington High Street
Buses	C1, 9, 10, 27, 28, 49 - Kensington High Street

WELLBEING
EAT

Down to Earth Café opened in August 2012 to the delight of the Kensington clientele who can't seem to get enough of the organic, vegetarian, vegan, raw and 'free from' menu. This combined café, deli and health food shop has also attracted a high calibre team of specialist chefs who cook (or hydrate in raw food chef Richard's case) breakfast, lunch, dinner, drinks and snacks every day of the week.

Raw foodists will love Richard's lasagne with meaty sundried tomatoes and pizzas made with almond, courgette, herb and flax seed base. And sweet-toothed dessert devotees will be spoilt for choice between Karen's sugar, wheat and dairy-free cakes, or a treat from the in-house (sugar and dairy free) sorbet making machine. There's also a menu of cooked dishes and daily special salads from health food chef, Marita.

Customers can continue their healthy eating habits by stocking up on organic brands and produce that line the shelves, saving themselves a trip to Whole Foods up the road and playing their part in making Down to Earth Kensington's favourite local health food haven.

TRIYOGA

372 King's Road, Chelsea SW3 5UZ
Tel: 020 7483 3344

WEST

Online	www.triyoga.co.uk @triyogauk
Hours	Mon to Fri: 9am to 9:30pm Sat & Sun: 9am to 6:30pm (check online for class times)
Average class price	£15 for a 90 minute class
Trains	Sloane Square / West Brompton
Buses	11, 22, 49, 319, 328, 345 - Beaufort Street

Despite an influx of new yoga studios opening in London of late, Triyoga continues to dominate the London yoga scene with the largest number of studios, classes and exceptionally experienced teachers.

Like it's three sister studios, the Chelsea space is typically Triyoga with three light and airy studios, all bedecked with white walls, the signature coloured windows in the Triyoga colours and filled with the delicious waft of incense. There's also a Pilates studio, three therapy rooms, a shop and in-house café serving vegetarian, raw and gluten-free post-class replenishment.

The Chelsea timetable has classes to suit all yoga students, be they beginners, Mums-to-be, marathon runners or morning Mysore practitioners. Whilst the drop-in classes are taught by local talent such as Bridget Woods Kramer, many international teachers make this their port of call when their schedules tour London, thus placing Triyoga firmly on the London yoga map with workshops and teacher trainings led by renowned teachers such as Kino Macgregor, Donna Fahri and John Scott.

EVOLVE WELLNESS CENTRE

10 Kendrick Mews, SW7 3HG
Tel: 020 7581 4090

WEST

Online	www.evolvewellnesscentre.com
	@evolvecentre
Hours	Mon-Fri: 9am-7pm
	Sat: 12.15-2.30pm
	Sun: 10.30am-12.45pm
	(check online for class times)
Average class price	£15 for a 60 min class
Trains	South Kensington
Buses	49, 70 - Queensbury Place or C1, 14, 74, 360, 430 South Kensington Tube station

WELLBEING RELAX

Tucked in the corner of a cobbled mews a few minutes walk from South Kensington tube station, Evolve Wellness is a centre that nourishes the soul, strengthens the body and inspires the mind.

Whilst yoga is a dominant fixture on Evolve's timetable and attracts some of London's much loved teachers, it's their emphasis on other holistic and self-developmental practices, community spirit and ecological endeavors which sets Evolve apart. As well as rolling out a yoga mat and taking a class in one of the three studio spaces, guests to the centre are also encouraged to explore other avenues of wellbeing. A day long meditation retreat, a 'living the law of attraction' workshop, a Shamanic healing session, or a 'herbs for health' talk are just a few of Evolve's offerings beyond the yoga realm.

Previously a private clinic, Evolve has been lovingly restored and revamped by founders Corinne and Adrian to create a space with a boutique feel and homely ambience, which is small enough to be personal and not in the least bit intimidating- yet large enough to disperse the 90 or so people that descend on the centre on one of their busy Monday evenings.

The three studio spaces are cosy without being cramped and studio one is a treat to practice in, with large Victorian windows letting in the light and the views of the outside mews. Artwork by local artists is dotted around the centre; there's a lounge area for hanging out with a herbal tea or catching up with classmates and a roof top garden which blossoms with Evolve's home-grown efforts at sustainability. There are also treatment rooms that offer everything from chiropractor appointments and massage, to the lesser known zero balancing and Shamanic healing. However, it's the centre's classroom which really sums up the aim of Evolve.

The belief that life should be lived to it's optimum potential beats at the heart of Evolve and is expressed through the classroom-based talks, workshops, courses and film screenings, which aspire to motivate and inspire attendees in self-growth. Evolve's emphasis on cultivating community and sustainability is also evident in the classroom, which hosts a monthly 'Sustainability Club', aiming to implement local initiatives and raise awareness of sustainability in South Kensington.

The diversity of practices, treatments and events on offer is testament to it's founders' own passions and pursuits. Ex-ballet dancer, turned life coach Corinne Blumm and her ex-fund analyst and entrepreneur partner, Adrian Kowal, make an inspiring pair whose passion for esoteric practices, thirst for self development and curiosity about life itself, ensure Evolve is by no means just another yoga studio.

THE LIFE CENTRE

15 Edge Street, Notting Hill W8 7PN
Tel: 020 7221 4602

Online	www.thelifecentre.com @thelifecentreuk
Hours	Mon-Fri: 8am-9.30pm Sat & Sun: 8am-7.30pm (check online for class times)
Average class price	£15 for a 90 min class
Trains	Notting Hill Gate
Buses	27, 52, 70, 328, 452 - Notting Hill Gate Tube

WEST

WELLBEING · *RELAX*

Set in a converted chapel on a quiet residential road in Notting Hill, The Life Centre is one of London's original yoga centres, providing yoga, Pilates, treatments and yoga therapy since 1993.

The centre has two studios – the larger downstairs studio holds a class of 27 and radiates light through ceiling skylights, whilst the second floor 'loft' studio holds an intimate class of 15 overlooking the rooftops of Notting Hill. Additionally, natural health therapists hire out the three therapy rooms, offering a variety of nourishing and invigorating treatments.

The Life Centre's Islington studio opened in 2011. As well as offering a busy timetable of classes and treatments, it also serves as the home for 'Yogacampus', the Life Centre's training and education arm.

Through Yogacampus, students and teachers can enroll on workshops, weekend intensives or the 18 month yoga teacher training programme. All Yogacampus trainings are taught by highly regarded and respected teachers from the UK and beyond, and cover a broad range of topics including yoga theory, therapy, practice, philosophy and anatomy.

RUN DEM CREW WEST

Paddington Recreational Ground, Maida Vale W9 1RX

Online	www.rundemcrew.com/rdcwest @rundemcrew
Hours	Every Monday Meet: 6.45pm, run: 7.15pm and finish: 8.15-8.30pm
Price	Free to attend
Trains	Maida Vale
Buses	16, 46, 98, 187, 332 - Hall Road

WEST

Run Dem Crew insists it isn't a running club. Instead, it's a collective of creative types, urban teenagers, aspiring athletes, first time 5k runners and just about anyone in between, who meet on a weekly basis to network, collaborate and support… all whilst running around London in unison.

Founded in 2007 by DJ, writer and poet Charlie Dark, Run Dem Crew has out-grown it's original Shoreditch meeting space and the ever-expanding Tuesday night crew and headed West to pound the pavements around Paddington on Monday nights.

Despite the crew's mantra to 'Go hard or go home', it's ensured that no one is ever left behind, so runners are split into groups according to fitness and pace. 'Tortoises' are aiming for a 10 minute mile, 'cheetahs' a speedy 7-8 minutes and the 'hares' and 'greyhounds' run in between.

But being a part of Run Dem Crew means a whole lot more than your minutes per mile. It's about contributing to the one-of-a-kind community that Dark has created, exploring London, grasping the opportunities it presents and most importantly - inspiring your crew to do the same.

SAGAR SOUTH INDIAN VEGETARIAN RESTAURANT

157 King Street, Hammersmith W6 9JT
www.sagarveg.co.uk
Hours: Mon-Thurs & Sun: 12pm-10.45pm,
Fri & Sat: 12pm-11.30pm
Trains: Ravenscourt Park Tube
Buses: 27, H91, 190, 391 - Dalling Road

BUMPKIN

209 Westbourne Park Road W11 1EA
www.bumpkinuk.com
Hours: Mon-Fri: 11am-11pm, Sat & Sun: 10am-11pm
Trains: Westbourne Park / Ladbroke Grove Tube
Buses: 28, 31, 328 - Shrewsbury Road / Brunel Estate

THE SPECIAL YOGA CENTRE

2a Wrentham Avenue NW10 3HA
www.specialyoga.org.uk
Hours: Mon & Fri: 10am-9.45pm,
Tues-Thurs:7am-9.30pm, Sat & Sun: 9am-8pm
Trains: Kensal Rise Overground
Buses: 6, 52, 187, 302 - Kensal Rise Station

IYENGAR YOGA INSTITUTE

223a Randolph Avenue W9 1NL
www.iyi.org.uk
Hours: Mon, Tues & Thurs: 9.30am-9.45pm,
Weds: 7am-9.30pm, Fri: 9.30am-8pm,
Sat: 8.15am-6.30pm, Sun: 9.30am-7.30pm
(or check online for class times)
Trains: Maida Vale Tube
Buses: 16, 31, 98, 316, 328, 332 - Carlton Vale

JIVAMUKTI YOGA

Unit 136-137, 300 Kensal Road W10 5BE
www.jivamuktiyogalondon.co.uk
Hours: Mon-Fri: 7am-8.30pm/9.45pm, Sat & Sun:
9am-6.30pm (or check online for class times)
Trains: Queens Park Rail, Overground & Tube
Buses: 18, 28, 228 - Fifth Avenue

NEW YORK PILATES STUDIO

Top Floor, 43-47 Lonsdale Rd. NW6 6RA
www.nypilates.co.uk
Hours: Mon-Sun. Check online for class times.
Trains: Queen's Park Overground Tube
Buses: 6, 36, 98, 187, 206 - Queen's Park Station

FRAME QUEEN'S PARK

27 Beethovern Street W10 4LG
www.moveyourframe.com/queens-park
Hours: Mon-Sun: Times vary from 6.45am-9.30pm
(check online for class times)
Trains: Queens Park Rail, Overground & Tube
Buses: 6, 187, 316 - Allington Road

WESTWAY SPORTS CENTRE

1 Crowthorne Road, W10 6RP
www.westwaysportscentre.org.uk
Hours: Mon-Fri: 7am-10pm, Sat: 7am-8pm,
Sun: 8am-9pm
Trains: Latimer Road / White City Tube
Buses: 295, 316 - Crowthorne Road
or 72, 95, 220 - Cavell House

YOGAAT

www.yogaat.com
33-34 Westpoint, Warple Way W3 0RG
Hours: Check online for class times
Trains: Acton Central Tube
Buses: 207, 266, 272 - Larden Road

SAF

www.safrestaurant.co.uk
The Barkers Building, 1st Floor,
Whole Foods Market, W8 5SE
Hours: Mon-Sat 12-10pm, Sun: 12-6pm
Trains: High Street Kensington
Buses: 9, 10, 27, 28, 49, 328 - High Street Kensington

EAST

BODY STUDIO

89a Rivington Street, Shoreditch EC2A 3AY
Tel: 020 7729 0111

Online	www.bodystudio.co.uk
	@bodystudioe2
Hours	Mon - Fri: 7am-9pm
	Sat: 9am-3pm
	Sun: Open for private bookings
Average class price	£12
Trains	Old Street / Shoreditch High Street
Buses	26, 47, 48 149, 77, 242 - Calvert Avenue

WELLBEING MOVE

Ensconced beneath railway arches, behind a buzz-on-entry door and with a boxing ring looming large, it would be easy to pass Body Studio off as yet another intimidating boxing club cliché. Far from it. Body Studio abolishes the burly stereotype of personal training and boxing gyms with a friendly atmosphere and a diverse holistic offering of programmes. Many of the resident trainers have been working there for years, building a great rapport and impressive results with their clients – most of whom hail from the creative, rather than corporate end of Shoreditch, bringing a cool and cutting edge energy to the space.

The boxing ring plays host to classes for all levels, in-house tournaments and is also the pop-up home of the hugely popular women's boxing collective 'Girls in Gloves', as well as 'Pink Collar' gay boxing nights. But it's not all right hooks and jabs - their holistic approach to fitness has ensured a packed timetable of yoga, cardio and martial art classes, which can be taken by non-members on a pay-as-you-go basis, or included in the price of a full membership.

FRAME

29 New Inn Yard, Shoreditch EC2A 3EY
Tel: 020 7033 1855

Online	www.moveyourframe.com
	@FRAMEShoreditch
Hours	Mon-Fri: 7am-9.30pm
	Sat: 9.30am-4.30pm
	Sun: 10am-6.30pm
Average class price	£12
Trains	Old Street / Shoreditch High Street
Buses	8, 26, 48, 67, 138, 242 - Shoreditch High Street Station

WELLBEING MOVE

Keeping the East London hipsters fitting into their skinny jeans since 2009, Frame is a dance, fitness, Pilates and holistic studio, that places fun and fast results high on the agenda. Forget slogging it out on the treadmill or committing to a contract, Frame's signature classes, bespoke bootcamps and weekend workshops will whip you into shape and can be taken on a pay as you go basis. However, unlimited monthly and annual memberships are also available for those who want to make the most of the 120 classes a week on Frame's timetable.

Nestled under the arches of the railway line just off Shoreditch High Street, Frame oozes signature East London style with exposed brickwork, rocking playlists and infectiously enthusiastic instructors filling the four studio spaces. Having proved a huge hit in Shoreditch, Frame opened the doors of their Queen's Park studio in May 2012, where signature Frame classes such as 'Bend it Like Barbie', 'Music Video Classics' and 'Happy Hour Yoga' are proving just as popular with West Londoners.

SHOREDITCH PILATES

First floor, 232 Shoreditch High Street E1 6PJ
Tel: 07817 604846

EAST

Online	www.shoreditchpilates.com @shoreditchbeing
Hours	Mon: 10am-8.30pm, Tues-Fri: 7.45am-8.30pm, Sat & Sun: 10am-12.30pm (check online for class times)
Average class price	£10
Trains	Liverpool Street / Shoreditch High Street
Buses	8, 26, 48, 78, 149 - Commercial St. / Worship St.

WELLBEING
MOVE

Fed up with the burgeoning costs of hiring a room to host her Pilates classes, teacher Laura Hogg sought out a space to call her own and in early 2011, Shoreditch Pilates was born.

The space comprises two studios adjoined by a small reception area that is creatively styled and finished with thoughtful touches that hint at Laura's previous career in visual merchandise. Studio one is home to mat-based Pilates and yoga classes, with floor to ceiling mirrors and a well-stocked shelf of Pilates and yoga props to help stretch and support you further into your poses. Studio two features three Pilates Reformer machines and offers challenging, yet hugely effective classes that will have you pulling springs and levers to discover and develop muscles you never knew existed.

Open seven days a week, Shoreditch Pilates offers morning, lunchtime and evening classes, providing E1 dwellers and city workers with a much needed oasis to relax, restore and build strength for another lively day in London.

LONDON BUDDHIST CENTRE

51 Roman Road, Bethnal Green E2 0HU
Tel: 0845 458 4716

EAST

Online	www.lbc.org.uk
Hours	Mon-Fri: 7am- 9.45pm Sat: 10am-5pm Sun: 10.15-11.30am (check class times online)
Average class price	£2-£8 donation
Trains	Bethnal Green / Cambridge Heath
Buses	D6, 8, 309 - Burnham Street or D3, 106, 388 - Bethnal Green Tube

Obliterated by the Blitz and the former stomping ground of the Krays, Bethnal Green doesn't necessarily conjure connotations of peace and tranquility. But upon slipping your shoes off and entering the London Buddhist Centre, the stresses and chaos of the city immediately melt away.

Walk through a secluded walled garden complete with soothing sounds of a water feature and garden benches for a contemplative perch, and into a bright and airy reception area, which also doubles up as a well-stocked Buddhist book shop. Further inside, the centre features four 'shrine' rooms, each filled with a large Buddha statue, fresh flowers, candles and incense for a subtle, yet stunning finish apt for the sacred meditations practiced within the centre. Each shrine room has plenty of meditation mats, cushions and straight-backed chairs to ensure practitioners are comfortably adopting correct meditation postures.

The centre's aim is to help as many people as possible deepen their experience of life's value and potential by introducing them to Buddhism and meditation. The centre is run on generosity alone, with all teachers and staff offering their time, skills and experience voluntarily, with regular donations ensuring charges are kept as low as possible. Thankfully, the London Buddhist Centre is a popular and thriving hub attracting the attendance (and hence donations) from Londoners from all walks of life.

Newcomers are warmly welcomed by the voluntary staff and mix with more experienced meditators to form an eclectic ensemble of practitioners, proving that Buddhism and meditation knows no boundaries or stereotypes. The centre offers drop-in sessions every lunchtime from 1-2pm (except Sunday), where for as little as a £2 donation, practitioners can learn and practice the 'mindfulness of breathing' or metta bhavana (loving kindness) techniques, which are taught on alternate days. For those that want to delve deeper, the centre offers longer evening sessions, courses, workshops, open days, festivals and poetry nights. Or, for a truly immersive integration into meditation, the centre offers retreats at 'Vajrasana', their purpose built centre in rural Suffolk, set over six acres of gardens and with communal living facilities, vegetarian meals and a stunning circular meditation shrine room.

In addition to events at their Bethnal Green base, London Buddhist Centre also run meditation and Buddhism classes and courses on Saturdays at their venue on St Martin's Lane near Covent Garden.

If your meditation session at Bethnal Green leaves you feeling peckish and the complimentary tea and biscuits on offer don't suffice, nip next door to the vegetarian deli 'The Larder' for home-made lunches and cake. Alternatively, you could mosey further down the road to 'Jambala', the second-hand Buddhist bookshop, to stock up on some inspiring reading to feed your meditation practice further.

LOOK MUM NO HANDS!

49 Old Street EC1V 9HX
Tel: 020 7253 1025

Online	www.lookmumnohands.com
	@1ookmumnohands
Hours	Mon–Fri: 7.30am-10.30pm
	Sat : 9am-10pm
	Sun:10am-10pm
Average price	£6 for lunch
Trains	Barbican / Old Street
Buses	55, 153, 243 - Aldersgate St. or 4, 56 - Clerkenwell Rd.

WELLBEING · EAT

Blame Bradley Wiggins or Boris bikes, London's cycling scene is growing at break neck speed. Thankfully, Look Mum No Hands resides on Old Street's bike commuter belt to feed, fix and unite London's pedaling fraternity.

Comprising a café bar and bicycle workshop, Look Mum serves up a menu of healthy and tasty cycling fuel that can be enjoyed whilst waiting for a bike repair or during any of the bike-inspired social events and live race screenings that take place a few evenings each week.

Daily deliveries of fresh fruit and vegetables are used for juices, smoothies, hot dishes and salads, whilst there's homemade cakes, Square Mile coffee and cider, ales and beers for those craving a treat after a day in the saddle. Ensuring that the bikes are as well looked after as their owners, there's also a regular bike maintenance course to keep your two wheels in tip top condition.

Occupying an ample sized space on Old Street that is filled with bikes and cycling paraphernalia adorning its walls, Look Mum No Hands is playing a pivotal part in placing London on the map of Europe's best cycling cities.

THE GALLERY CAFÉ

21 Old Ford Road, Bethnal Green E2 9PL
Tel: 020 8980 2091

Online	thegallerycafe.wordpress.com
	@The_GalleryCafe
Hours	Mon-Fri: 8am-9pm
	Sat & Sun: 9am-9pm
Average price	£6 for a meal
Trains	Bethnal Green / Cambridge Heath
Buses	D3, 106, 309, 388 - York Hall

WELLBEING · EAT

Perfectly placed between York Hall's gym, pool and spa and yoga studio 'Yoganesh', The Gallery Café serves up vegetarian fare and a schedule of in-house events that keep this a thriving hub of wellbeing on Old Ford Road.

Offering vegan versions of all their vegetarian dishes, the Gallery Café's menu features full veggie breakfasts with tasty tofu scramble (sourced from neighbouring Brick Lane tofu supplier, Clean Bean), delicious freshly made pizzas and home-made vegan cakes – all of which can be enjoyed whilst sinking into one of their ample sofas with the Sunday papers, catching some rays in the sun-trap conservatory or on the outdoor terrace. The menu changes on a seasonal and daily basis, swapping hearty stews, soups and curries in the winter for fresh salads in the summer months and offering freshly prepared sandwiches, wraps and pizzas all year round. Coffee connoisseurs will appreciate the serving of Nude coffee, locally roasted at Brick Lane's Truman Brewery, or there's Teapigs tea, freshly made juice or organic beer and wine for those wanting something a little more thirst-quenching.

As part of St Margaret's House, a charity which provides space for local organisations, projects and small charities, The Gallery Café wholeheartedly contribute to the Tower Hamlets community, utilising their later opening hours and alcohol license with a packed evening agenda of affordable music, film, visual arts, poetry and comedy nights, which are performed by local talent and raise funds to invest back into St Margaret's House. Highlights include the monthly Gallery Café book club and weekly Monday night screenings in the Chapel cinema at the back of the café, which are open to anyone to attend. There's fun and fundraising opportunities to be had during the daylight hours too, with a summer series of children's book parties, garden games and community days taking place in the Gallery Café garden every weekend throughout July and August.

Staying true to their name, the café's walls are adorned with the work of local artists, which change on the first Thursday of every month, when crowds of art appreciators following Time Out's First Thursdays series descend on The Gallery Café to check out the latest exhibition alongside a vegan cupcake or organic ale.

With such an extensive offering of events, if would be easy for the café's schedule to surpass it's menu, but thanks to the commitment and passion of their chefs and waiting staff (most of whom are vegetarian and many of whom volunteer their time to the cause) who deliver delicious, locally sourced and enticing meals, The Gallery Café remains the place of choice for wifi-seeking freelancers, group get-togethers, hungry yogis, swimmers, gym goers and runners, who can grab a healthy bite in a home from home environment.

YORK HALL

Old Ford Road, Bethnal Green E2 9PJ
Tel: 020 8709 5845

Online	www.better.org.uk/leisure/york-hall-leisure-centre/ www.spa-london.org @spalondon
Hours	Mon-Fri: 7am-9.30pm Sat: 8am-9.30pm Sun: 8am-7.30pm
Average class price	£4.50 for a swim, £24 for a 3 hour thermal spa
Trains	Bethnal Green / Cambridge Heath
Buses	D3, 106, 309, 388 - York Hall

WELLBEING RELAX

Previously one of Britain's best loved boxing venues, York Hall has benefitted from several revamps in recent years but is still rich with the history and heritage it has accumulated since it opened in 1929.

The 1,200 seater theatre has played host to boxing matches, pool competitions, fashion shows and the odd episode of BBC's The Apprentice, whilst the 33 meter swimming pool has seen synchronised swimmers and London 2012 Olympians training in it's lanes. But casual gym-goers and non-Olympians be assured - members of the public are warmly welcomed to use the excellent facilities in the gym and the swimming pool, both on a drop-in or membership basis. Owned by Tower Hamlets Council, York Hall was threatened with closure in 2004, so underwent a £1.3m refurbishment which saw it's original Turkish bathhouse in the basement transformed into 'Spa London'; an affordable day spa complete with beauty, body and spa treatments.

LISTINGS

OTHER EAST LONDON WELLBEING DESTINATIONS

HEALTHY STUFF E8

168 Dalston Lane E8 1NG
www.healthystuffe8.co.uk
Hours: Mon-Fri: 8am-7pm, Sat: 10am-6pm,
Sun: 10am-5pm
Trains: Dalston Kingsland / Dalston Kingsland /
Hackney Central
Buses: 30, 56 - Cecilia Road / Greenacre Court

THE LARDER

241-243 Globe Road Bethnal Green E2 0JD
www.worldslarder.co.uk
Hours: Mon-Fri: 8am-7pm, Sat: 9am-5pm,
Sun: 9am-4pm
Trains: Bethnal Green Tube /
Cambridge Heath Overground
Buses: D6, 8, 309 - Burnham Street
or D3, 106, 388 - Bethnal Green Tube

THE GROCERY

54-56 Kingsland Road E2 8DP
www.thegroceryshop.co.uk
Hours: Mon-Sun: 8am-10pm
Trains: Hoxton Overground / Old Street Tube
Buses: 67, 149, 242, 243 - Falkirk Street

AMICO BIO

44 Cloth Fair City of London EC1A 7JQ
www.amicobio.co.uk
Hours: Mon-Fri: 12-10.30pm, Sat: 5pm-10.30pm,
Sun: Closed
Trains: Barbican Tube / Farringdon Tube
Buses: 4, 153 - Barbican Tube Station

AERIAL YOGA LONDON

30 New Road Whitechapel E1 2AX
www.aerialyogalondon.co.uk
Hours: Tues-Sun. Check online for class times.
Trains: Whitechapel Tube
Buses: D3, 15, 115, 135 - New Road

YOGA PLACE

www.yogaplace.co.uk
1st Floor 449-453 Bethnal Green Road E2 9QH
Hours: Mon-Fri: 6am-9.30pm, Sat: 8.30am-1.30pm,
Sun: 8.30am-7.15pm
Trains: Bethnal Green Tube
Buses: D3, D6, 8, 106, 388 - Bethnal Green Tube

YOGA ON THE LANE

www.yogaonthelane.com
105 Shacklewell Lane Dalston, London E8 2EB
Mon: 12.30-9pm, Tues-Thurs: 7.15am-9pm,
Fri & Sat: 9am-1.30pm, Sun: 10am-1pm
Trains: Rectory Road Rail /
Dalston Kingsland Overground
Buses: 67, 76, 236, 276, 488 - Shacklewell Lane

SHINE HOLISTIC

52 Stoke Newington Church Street N16 0NB
www.shineholistic.co.uk
Hours: Mon-Fri: 10am-9pm, Sat: 10am-6pm,
Sun: 11am-5pm
Trains: Stoke Newington Rail
Buses: 73, 393, 476 - Bouverie Road

HOLISTIC HEALTH

www.holistichealthhackney.co.uk
64 Broadway Market E8 4QJ
Hours: Mon – Thurs: 9am-9pm,
Fri & Sat: 9am-4pm Sun:11am-1pm
Trains: London Fields Rail/Haggerston Overground
Buses: 236, 394 - Broadway Market
or 26, 48, 55, 254 - St Joseph's Hospice

ONE LIFE PERSONAL TRAINING STUDIO

www.onelifepersonaltraining.co.uk
19-20 Barn Street London N16 0JT
Hours: Mon-Fri: 7am-8pm. Check online for
evening and weekend class times.
Trains: Stoke Newington Rail
Buses: 76, 393, 476 - Stoke Newington Town Hall

MILE END CLIMBING WALL

www.mileendwall.org.uk
Haverfield Road E3 5BE
Hours: Mon-Thurs: 12-9.30pm, Fri: 12-9pm,
Sat & Sun: 10am-6pm
Trains: Mile End Tube
Buses: D6, 277, 339, 425 - Arbery Road

CLISSOLD LEISURE CENTRE & POOL

www.better.org.uk/leisure/clissold-leisure-centre

63 Clissold Road Stoke Newington N16 9EX

Hours: Mon-Fri: 7am-10pm, Sat: 8am-7pm

Sun: 8am-5pm

Trains: Canonbury Overground/ Rectory Road Rail

Buses: 73, 476 - Barbauld Road

LONDON FIELDS LIDO

www.better.org.uk/leisure/london-fields-lido

London Fields West Side, Hackney E8 3EU

Hours: Mon-Fri:7.15am-6pm, Sat: 8am-5pm

Sun: 8am-5pm

Trains: London Fields Rail/Haggerston Overground

Buses: 236, 394 - Broadway Market

or 26, 48, 55, 254 - St Thomas's Square

LONDON FIGHT FACTORY

www.londonfightfactory.com

LFF E2, 16-22 Pritchard's Road E2 9AP

Hours: Mon-Fri: 12.30-9.30pm, Sat 10.30am-2pm

Trains: Cambridge Heath Rail /

Bethnal Green Tube

Buses: 26, 48, 55 - Hackney Road

YOGANESH

www.yoganesh.co.uk

27 Old Ford Road, Bethnal Green E2 9PJ

Hours: Mon-Sun (check online for class times)

Trains: Bethnal Green Tube /

Cambridge Heath Rail

Buses: D3, 106, 309, 388 - York Hall

NORTH

INSPIRAL

250 Camden High Street NW1 8QS
Tel: 020 7428 5875

Online	www.inspiralled.net @inspiralled
Hours	Mon-Thur: 9am-10pm Fri & Sat: 9am-2am Sun: 9am-11.30pm
Average price	£8 for a main course
Trains	Camden Town / Camden Road
Buses	C2, 46, 88, 134, 168, 214 - Camden Gardens

WELLBEING EAT

Despite a saturation of food stalls whose flavours of world cuisine waft through Camden market, few can entice Camden crowds away from Inspiral - the living food lounge that serves up fine vegan fare, canal views and late night music and performance events.

One of the leaders of the London raw and vegan scene, Inspiral opened in 2007 having evolved from 'IDSpiral', a festival chill out area. Although Inspiral stay true to their festival origins with open mic nights, live performances and DJs, it is their vegan menu that is the headline act. Passionately vegan, the Inspiral team boost their menu with superfoods, tonic herbs and life enhancing techniques of food preparation. Raw pizza, vegan ice cream and sprouted seed salads are a few of the favourites on the menu, best washed down with the award-winning 'Banana Karma' smoothie or a glass of organic wine. Having recently launched wholesale distribution of some of their raw snacks and with designs on a fleet of vegan ice-cream vans, it's unlikely Inspiral will be confined to Camden for much longer.

THE GATE

370 St John Street, Islington EC1V 4NN
Tel: 020 7278 5483

NORTH

Online	www.thegaterestaurants.com
	@gaterestaurant
Hours	Mon-Sun: 12pm-11pm
Average class price	£12 for a main course
Trains	Angel / Old Street
Buses	153, 341, 19, 38 - St John Street / Goswell Road

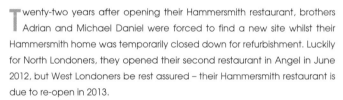

WELLBEING · EAT

Twenty-two years after opening their Hammersmith restaurant, brothers Adrian and Michael Daniel were forced to find a new site whilst their Hammersmith home was temporarily closed down for refurbishment. Luckily for North Londoners, they opened their second restaurant in Angel in June 2012, but West Londoners be rest assured – their Hammersmith restaurant is due to re-open in 2013.

Despite a plethora of bars and restaurants on Islington's Upper Street, none of them specifically cater for vegetarians. Furthermore, very few of them can boast the amazing flavours that are luring both vegetarians and meat eaters alike to The Gate on St John's Street, which straddles the borders of Clerkenwell and Angel.

The Gate's menu pays homage to the traditional Indian, Arabic and Jewish dishes Adrian and Michael were fed by their Grandmother, and is honed by a team of top chefs who whilst not strictly vegetarian, are proudly passionate about serving only the very best veggie dishes .

Although Indo-Iraqi in origin, the menu is defined as 'world cuisine', combining flavours and dishes from all corners of the globe, such as Mexican Huevos Rancheros for brunch, zingy Thai salad for dinner and an Anglicised apple, rhubarb and ginger crumble for dessert. Approved by the Vegetarian Society, The Gate is meticulous about serving 100% vegetarian produce, even using vegetarian alternatives to parmesan cheese (which isn't actually vegetarian as it's made using calf rennet.)

Co-owner Adrian Daniel states "We like the ingredients to do the talking", but in fact the presentation and aesthetic appeal of the dishes are on a par with their taste. Whether it's the multi-layered corn and polenta cake with artichokes, aubergine, sweet potatoes and tomatoes stacked into a lofty food tower, or the painstakingly arranged halloumi kibi, the food formations of the menu elicit broad smiles from diners and provide salivating photographic fodder for The Gate's own cookery books.

The menu is so enticing and the food so flavoursome, carnivores will barely notice the lack of meat. But if they do, they can drown their sorrows with a 'horseradish and watercress crush' or 'carrot and coriander souffle' cocktail – just a couple of tempting creations to be found on the drinks menu.

Set in a bright and airy split-level space that curves around a bar, The Gate has done well to secure a venue that suits the restaurant's clean and wholesome menu, whilst offering a prime location and relaxed ambience. With attributes like these there is little doubt that many diners will succumb to the 'everything in moderation' attitude to healthy eating - making the most of the delicious desserts and drinks menu well in to the later hours.

ITADAKI-ZEN

139 Kings Cross Road WC1X 9BJ
Tel: 020 7278 3573

Online	www.itadakizen.com
Hours	Lunch: Mon, Tues, Thurs & Fri: 12pm-14.30pm Dinner: Mon-Thurs 6-10pm Fri & Sat: 6-10.30pm
Average price	£14 for a main course
Trains	Kings Cross
Buses	17, 30, 73, 205, 214, 476 - Kings Cross Road

WELLBEING EAT

Meaning 'to take the food of life' (Itadaki) and to 'fix or mend' (Zen), Itadaki-Zen applies an ancient Eastern philosophy to food, which draws on it's natural medicinal properties to achieve optimum health and a closer connection to one's spirit.

Enlightenment through food may seem like an ambitious and far-reaching aim for a small vegan Japanese restaurant in Kings Cross, but if any cuisine is going to cleanse you of the indulgences of the Western diet and bring you closer to your spirit, it's Itadaki-Zen. Dishes are homemade, slowly prepared to maintain all the healing and health-giving properties of the produce and follow macrobiotic principles, predominantly featuring rice, root vegetables, seaweeds and soy beans. Head chef Keiko cites healing sushi and vegetable harumaki as two of the most popular dishes.

Affiliated with Japan's 'Academy for Agricultural Philosophy', Itadaki-Zen also serves as a training centre to spread awareness of this startlingly simple, yet incredibly effective attitude to eating.

COOKIES & SCREAM

Unit L1, Dingwalls Gallery, Camden Lock Place NW1 8AF
Tel: 020 8444 9944

Online	www.cookiesandscream.com @cookiesscream
Hours	Mon to Fri: 9am to 9:30pm Sat & Sun: 9am to 6:30pm
Average price	£2.50 for a cookie
Trains	Camden Town / Camden Road / Chalk Farm
Buses	24 , 27, 31, 168 - Camden Market

NORTH

WELLBEING EAT

When shopping fatigue strikes at Camden Market, Cookies & Scream are on hand to perk you up with a hit of vegan and gluten-free sweetness that will see you through to that final bargain of the day.

Founded by a couple comprising a gluten-intolerant wife and vegan husband, Cookies & Scream has grown from a home bakery in Muswell Hill to a permanent stall at Camden Market. Today, they fill the Dingwalls gallery with the sweet smell of freshly baked brownies and peanut butter cookies seven days a week.

Priding themselves on bakes which taste devilish but are made from angelic ingredients, the self-titled 'cookie crew' use only the finest ingredients – including coconut oil, agave syrup and rice flour - in their low-fat and dairy, egg, wheat and gluten-free bakes.

You can grab a cookie, cake or muffin to go, or settle down in their seating area with a freshly brewed cuppa and watch the captivating chaos of Camden pass by.

MILKSHAKES EGGG ALL THE BOYS
OUR YARD.. DAMN RIGHT THEY'RE
& LOW FAT & SWEETENED WITH
AGAVE!

OLD SKOOL VANILLA SCREAM £2.50

HAROUN'S ESPRESSO SHAKE £3

GOSH BROWNIE SCREAM £3.50
SHAKE

PEANUT BUTTER CHIQUITA SHAKE
AND REALLY COOL DRINKS FOR
HOT BABES

ICED AMERICANO   £1.60
ICED LATTE   £1.80
ICED MOCHA LOCA   £2.00
w/ REAL CHOCOLA

TIME FOR TEA

COOKIES AND SCREAM

SKOOL BAKES AND HOTSTUFF

AWARD WINNING BAKEHOUSE   ALL PRODUCTS VEGAN AND GLUTEN FREE

ALCHEMY

Unit 101, Stables Market, Chalk Farm Road, Camden NW1 8AH
Tel: 020 7267 6188

Online	www.alchemythecentre.co.uk
	@alchemythecentre
Hours	Mon- Fri: 7am-10pm,
	Sat & Sun: 9am-7.30pm
Average class price	£15 for a 90 minute class
Trains	Camden Town / Camden Road / Chalk Farm
Buses	24 , 27, 31, 168 - Camden Market

WELLBEING RELAX

Less of a yoga studio and more of a 'centre for transformation', Alchemy offers contemporary and ancient methods of healing to align mind, body and soul. With over 70 yoga classes on the timetable, yoga plays an important part at Alchemy but it's their additional emphasis on meditation and esoteric activities that gives Alchemy it's holistic and somewhat mystical edge.

Founded four years ago by a trio of yoga and business brains and housed in one of the historic Camden market stables, Alchemy combines classes with talks, workshops and treatments to offer a truly immersive esoteric experience. Astrology, reiki, metatronic healing and gong meditation classes sit on the timetable alongside the usual array of yoga styles and take place in the 'circle room' – a studio space specifically for inner reflection. The 'yoga room' is Alchemy's second studio space and home to a busy schedule of classes, including jivamukti, yin, hatha and ashtanga.

Kundalini yoga is a popular choice amongst Alchemy practitioners and hence a daily feature on the timetable, offered as classes in kundalini yoga or more specialist gong or shakti kundalini classes.

Beyond the studio class timetable there are kirtan concerts, movie nights, shakti dance, inspiration talks, reiki attunement and moon meditations to keep Alchemy's devoted clientele on their path. The variety of esoteric events on offer attract teachers, therapists and authors from all over the world, connecting an eclectic and international gathering.

The therapy rooms offer another space for transformation, where guests can enjoy treatments such as Tibetan honey massage, shamanic healing and aromatherapy massages. The in-house Alchemy café serves mouth-watering vegan and vegetarian fare seven days a week and provides café seating for visitors to the centre to check in with emails, meet fellow class mates, or even make a group booking to host a birthday bash. As expected, the menu is nutritious, virtuous and incredibly tasty. Superfoods spirulina and macca are on hand to enhance juices and smoothies and there are raw chocolate treats for a post-class pick-me-up.

The Alchemy shop sits alongside the café selling books, DVDs, equipment, products from the in-house spa and gorgeous yoga-inspired jewellery to enhance your yoga and meditation interests beyond Alchemy itself.

Set amongst the throngs of Camden market, it's a testament to the people and practices at Alchemy that produce such a serene ambiance that's immediately absorbed upon walking through the door. For spiritual seekers craving more than a yoga class, Alchemy's spell-binding array of transformative experiences is bound to leave them spoilt for choice.

MOVING ARTS BASE

134 Liverpool Road, Islington N1 1LA
Tel: 020 7609 6969

NORTH

Online	www.movingartsbase.eu @movingartsbase
Hours	Mon-Fri: 9am-9:30pm Sat & Sun: 9am-6:30pm
Average class price	£8-10
Trains	Angel / Highbury & Islington
Buses	4, 19, 43 - St Mary's Church

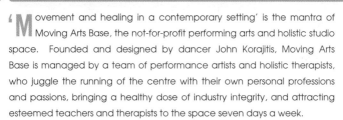

WELLBEING MOVE

'**M**ovement and healing in a contemporary setting' is the mantra of Moving Arts Base, the not-for-profit performing arts and holistic studio space. Founded and designed by dancer John Korajitis, Moving Arts Base is managed by a team of performance artists and holistic therapists, who juggle the running of the centre with their own personal professions and passions, bringing a healthy dose of industry integrity, and attracting esteemed teachers and therapists to the space seven days a week.

Tango, tai chi, jivamukti yoga and jazz dance are just a handful of classes on offer, whilst the therapy rooms are home to over fifty therapists offering an array of treatments including hypnotherapy, reflexology, massage and psychotherapy. Unlike some other dance and holistic spaces around London, Moving Arts Base choose function over grandeur and accessibility over indulgence, priding themselves on hiring the studios and therapy rooms at affordable prices, despite the premium N1 location. But don't confuse reasonable hire prices for shoddy spaces - John Korajitis has designed a truly beautiful space that's a treat to perform and practice in.

CASTLE CLIMBING CENTRE

Green Lanes, Stoke Newington N4 2HA
Tel: 020 8211 7720

Online	www.castle-climbing.co.uk @CastleClimbing
Hours	Mon-Fri: 12-10pm Sat & Sun: 10am-7pm
Average price	1 hour taster climb £20 Registered climbers £12 per visit
Trains	Manor House / Finsbury Park / Harringay
Buses	141, 341 - Lordship Park or 29, 253, 254 - Finsbury Park

WELLBEING MOVE

Formerly the Stoke Newington water pumping station, Castle Climbing Centre looms large on North London's Green Lanes in a majestic 1850's building strongly resembling a medieval castle. Open to the public since 1995, this Hackney landmark has become the premier indoor climbing centre in the South East, welcoming more climbers than any other centre in the UK.

Currently thriving in popularity, indoor climbing offers a physical challenge and a more mentally stimulating and sociable alternative to the gym or other slightly monotonous fitness pursuits. And whilst the Castle Climbing centre will help hone your skills for alfresco ascents on real mountains, sticking with indoor climbing alone is a worthy activity in itself, as Sport England statistics reveal that indoor climbing will overtake its outdoor counterpart within the next twelve months.

Spread over two floors, the centre houses over 450 routes, plenty of bouldering surfaces to play with and a 100ft tower (originally the castle's boiler chimney) to abseil down. Although busy during peak hours, there are enough walls, caves and quarries in this 1,200 square foot space for everyone.

In contrast to it's gothic austere exterior, Castle Climbing reeks colour inside, with artificial rock faces and the wall-fixed anchors painted in all the colours of the rainbow. Although the staff place paramount importance on health and safety, that doesn't stand in the way of the infectiously fun and social atmosphere at the centre. The Castle Café is a similarly enjoyable continuum of the climbing area, serving organic drinks, snacks and main courses made with fruit, vegetables and herbs from the Castle's own garden.

For those completely new to climbing, the £20 taster session is the perfect opportunity to be guided through your first climbing experience, where you'll be shown the ropes, anchors and plenty more climbing know-how in a fun, but reassuringly safe sixty minutes. If all goes well on the taster, there are six types of introductory courses, either spread over a few weeks or condensed into a weekend, followed by advanced masterclasses, one-on-one training and climbing holidays in Spain. Registered climbers can climb unsupervised and are allowed to bring in two novice climbers each.

Proving the mass appeal of indoor climbing, the Castle caters for kids with it's 'Gecko' children's climbing school that runs birthday parties, school holiday courses and personal tuition. For girls who fancy a night of boy-free bouldering, 'Women with Altitude' is a women-only monthly bouldering meet-up.

For a building that was initially built to pump water into East London in the 1800s, the Castle Climbing Centre is another shining example of wellbeing flowing in to the fabric of London.

LISTINGS
OTHER NORTH LONDON WELLBEING DESTINATIONS

MOTHER EARTH
282-284 Saint Paul's Road N1 2LH
www.motherearth-health.com
Hours: Mon-Fri 8am-8pm, Sat: 9am-7pm
Sun: 10am-6pm
Trains: Highbury & Islington Tube & Overground
Buses: 4, 19, 30, 271, 277, 393 - St Paul's Road /
Highbury Corner

VEGAN CROSS
73 Caledonian Road N1 9BT
www.vegancross.com
Hours: Mon: 11am -7.30pm
Tues - Sun: 10am-6.30pm
Trains: Kings Cross Rail & Tube
Buses: 71, 91, 259, 390 - Kings Cross Station /
Pentonville Road

OTTOLENGHI
287 Upper Street N1 2TZ
www.ottolenghi.co.uk
Hours: Mon-Sat: 8am-11pm, Sun: 9am-7pm
Trains: Highbury & Islington Tube / Angel Tube
Buses: 4, 19, 30, 43 - St Mary's Church

MANNA CUISINE

4 Erskine Road, Primrose Hill NW3 3AJ

www.mannav.com

Hours: Tues-Fri: 6.30-10.30pm

Sat & Sun: 12pm-10.30pm

Trains: Chalk Farm Tube / Camden Town Tube

Buses: 31, 168, 274, 393 - Chalk Farm Station

LONDON MEDITATION

www.london-meditation.co.uk

The Penthouse, 89 – 95 Parkway, Camden NW1 7PP

Hours: Varies - Check online for class times

Trains: Camden Town

Buses: C2, 274, Parkway or 24, 27, 31, 88 - Camden Town

LONDON CENTRE OF INDIAN CHAMPISSAGE

494 Caledonian Road N7 9RP

www.indianchampissage.com

Hours: Mon-Fri: 10am-7.30pm, Sat: 10am-5.30pm

Sun: By prior appointment.

Trains: Holloway Road Tube / Caledonian Road Tube

Buses: 17, 91, 259, 393 - Hillmarton Road

NATURA DAY SPA

64a Hampstead High Street NW3 1QH

www. naturadayspa.com

Hours: Tues, Weds & Sat: 9am-7pm, Thurs & Fri:

9am-7pm, Sun: 11am-5pm

Trains: Hampstead Tube

Buses: 46, 286, 603 - Hampstead Tube Station

YOGA JUNCTION

The Old Flower Shop, 93a Weston Park N8 9PR
www.yogajunction.co.uk
Hours: Mon-Sun. Check online for class times.
Trains: Hornsey Rail / Harringay Rail
Buses: W5, 41, 91 - Tottenham Lane YMCA

YOGAMATTERS YOGA SHOP

32 Clarendon Road N8 0DJ
www.yogamatters.com
Hours: Mon-Fri: 10am-5pm
Trains: Turnpike Lane Tube / Hornsey Rail
Buses: 144, 184, 230 - Turnpike Lane bus station

NORTH LONDON BUDDHIST CENTRE

72 Holloway Road N7 8JG
www.northlondonbuddhistcentre.com
Hours: Mon-Thurs: 12-7pm, Fri: 12-2pm,
Sat:11am-2.30pm
Trains: Holloway Road Tube / Drayton Park Rail
Buses: 43, 53, 271, 393 - Liverpool Road

SHAOLIN TEMPLE UK

207a Junction Road N19 5QA
www.shaolintempleuk.org
Hours: Mon-Fri: 6-9am, 4.30-1pm, Sun: 10am-1pm
Trains: Tufnell Park Tube / Archway Tube
Buses: 134, 390 - Monnery Road
or C11, 17, 41 - Archway Station

THE FACTORY FITNESS & DANCE CENTRE

407 Hornsey Road N19 4DX
www.factorylondon.com
Hours: Mon, Thur: 8am-10pm, Tues & Wed:
9.30am-10pm, Fri: 9.30am-9pm, Sat: 9.30am-7pm,
Sun: 9.30am-6pm (or check online for class times)
Trains: Upper Holloway Overground / Crouch Hill
Overground
Buses: 41, 91, 210 - Hornsey Road

SWISS COTTAGE LEISURE CENTRE

Adelaide Road NW3 3NF
**www.better.org.uk/leisure/swiss-cottage-leisure-
centre**
Hours: Mon-Fri: 6.30am-10pm, Sat & Sun: 8am-6pm
Trains: Swiss Cottage Tube
Buses: C11, DF2, 13, 31, 82, 113 - Swiss Cottage
Station

HAMPSTEAD HEATH SWIMMING PONDS

**Parliament Hill, Staffyard Highgate Road,
Hampstead Heath NW5 1QR**
www.hampsteadheath.net
Hours: Mon-Sun: 7/8am-sunset
Trains: Gospel Oak Overground / Tufnell Park Tube
Buses: C2, C11, 214 - William Ellis School

SOUTH

PING! TABLE TENNIS

The Marlborough Playground, 11-25 Union Street SE1 1LB
Tel: 0207 936 3131

Online	www.pingengland.co.uk
	@ping_tweets
Hours	Mon-Sun: 7.30am-sunset
	(varies throughout the year)
Average class price	Free
Tubes	Borough
Buses	21, 35, 40, 133, 343 - Union Street

WELLBEING
MOVE

A Sport England initiative funded with over £500,000 of National Lottery investment, Ping is on a mission to spread social table tennis, with free-to-use table tennis tables, bats and balls dotted around the capital. Whilst some of the 'pop-up' tables are only available during the summer months, Borough's Marlborough Place playground is home to three of Ping's permanent tables, which are readily used for impromptu knock-abouts and tournaments by local residents and office workers.

Having proved popular in London, Ping's tables have spread to Bristol and Liverpool, where Ping players are also enjoying coaching sessions from the English Table Tennis Association and Midnight Ping - with glow in the dark balls. Ping pong is enjoying something of a revival in the last few years, with East London hipster haunts Rich Mix and The Book Club, both hosting weekly tournaments. Having become established as an Olympic sport with worldwide popularity, the prevalence of Ping! tables around London is a self-congratulatory nod to the fact that ping pong did indeed begin in the 1890's as an English parlour game played on the dining room table.

HOT BIKRAM YOGA

1A Magdalen Street SE1 2EN
Tel: 020 7036 3855

Online	www.hotbikramyoga.co.uk @hotbikramyoga
Hours	Mon-Sun - See website for exact class times
Average class price	£20 for first 20 days £16.50 per session thereafter or monthly memberships available
Tubes	London Bridge
Buses	RV1, 47, 343 - Tooley Street / City Hall

WELLBEING RELAX

Love it or loathe it, there's no denying the popularity of Bikram yoga amongst Londoners. Having opened three Hot Bikram Yoga studios in South London over a seven year spell, studio owner and head teacher Olga Allon is proof that there's big business in Bikram.

This distinct style of yoga is named after it's founder, Bikram Choundary, who devised a 90 minute sequence of 26 postures, each practiced twice and in a room heated to a sweltering 40 °C. For first timers, the only aim is to withstand the heat and stay in the room for the duration of the class. For the more experienced there's never-ending challenges to be overcome through the sweat-inducing balancing, stretching and twisting postures.

With other studios in Fulham and Balham, the London Bridge space is the newest addition and the flagship of the trio. Testament to founder Olga's previous career as an architect, London Bridge is a sophisticated space, designed with features to keep the studio clean, hygienic and aesthetically appealing in it's sweaty state.

AYURVEDA PURA

48 Newton Lodge, Oval Square SE10 0BA
Tel: 0208 312 8383

Online	www.ayurvedapura.com
	@AyurvedaPura
Hours	Mon-Fri: 10am-8pm
	Sat: 9am-6pm, Sun: 10am-5pm
Average treatment price	£55 for a 60 minute treatment
Tubes	North Greenwich
Buses	108, 129, 132, 472 , 486 - Millennium Village

WELLBEING
RELAX

An academy, spa and yoga studio all in one, Ayurveda Pura is founded on Ayurveda - the 5,000 year old Indian holistic health system of physical, mental and emotional health - and applies these ancient methods to cure or relieve the modern day ailments of their city dwelling clientele. Just a short walk away from North Greenwich tube, it's almost ironic that the skyline of Canary Wharf looms large over the centre that seeks to cure such stresses of the corporate and modern world.

Depending on their aims or ailments, clients can chose from an abundance of treatments to balance their *dosha* (body type) back to full health, be it with a bespoke massage, facial, herbal remedy, a diet and lifestyle consultation or a 9 day long detoxing 'Panchakarma' treatment.

All practitioners working at the centre hold a degree or similar accreditation in Ayurveda, so high standards and expert integrity are guaranteed. The centre also serves as a training academy, welcoming students from far and wide to their diploma course, workshops and one-on-one training.

YOGAHAVEN

63 Wingate Square, Clapham Old Town SW4 0AF
Tel: 020 8617 0027

Online	yogahaven.co.uk/clapham @yogahaven
Hours	Mon-Fri: 6.30am-9.30pm Sat 8am-6pm, Sun: 8.30am- 7.30pm (check online for class times)
Average class price	£14 for a 60 minute class
Tubes	Clapham Common
Buses	88, 322, 417 - Clapham Common Old Town or 35, 37, 50, 155 - Clapham Common Tube

WELLBEING · RELAX

Founded by Allie Hill, a former teacher and practitioner of Bikram yoga, Yogahaven offers yoga flow, ashtanga, jivamukti, kundalini and pregnancy classes – some of which are taught upstairs in room temperature studio 1, with others taught downstairs in studio 2 which is heated to a toasty 40 degrees.

Although in agreement with Bikram Choundry on hot yoga's ability to stretch muscles deeper and more safely and to promote sweating and circulation, Yogahaven's classes are based on a unique style called leela (meaning 'play' in Sanskrit), which informs more intuitive and spontaneous sequences of postures than those practiced in Bikram yoga.

The Clapham studio hosts 6 to 7 classes every day of the week and feaures a shop selling yoga gear - including Lululemon, of which founder Allie Hill is an ambassador - and spacious changing facilities for the compulsory post hot yoga shower. There are also studios in Brighton, Birmingham and a few stops up the Northern line in Islington, for those who stray beyond SW4.

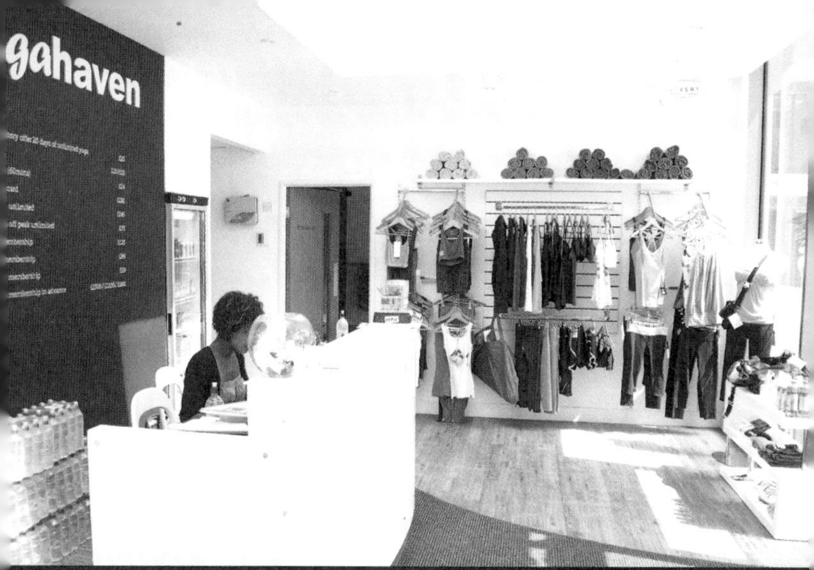
gahaven

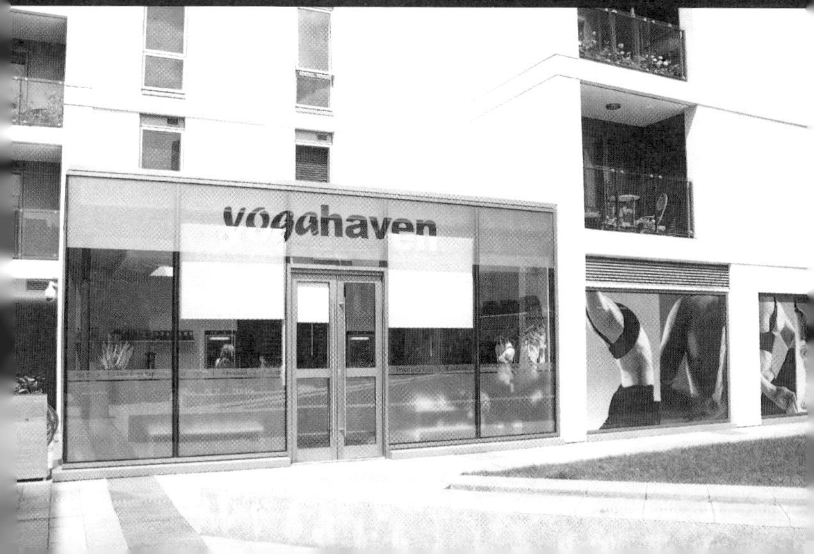
yogahaven

SHAMBHALA CENTRE

27 Belmont Close, Clapham SW4 6AY
Tel: 020 7720 3207

Online	www.shambhala.org.uk
Hours	Public meditation on Mon & Weds 7.30-9.30pm & pre-booked courses throughout the week and at weekends
Average class price	Suggested donation of £3 for a drop-in class
Tubes	Clapham Common
Buses	50, 88, 155, 322, 345 - St Luke's Avenue

WELLBEING
RELAX

Part of the international Shambhala community, the London Shambhala Centre provides instructions, classes, courses, retreats and talks in meditation, Buddhism and the meditative arts. Originating from a Tibetan Buddhism lineage, the Shambhala tradition encourages us to live in a heightened state of wakefulness, which in turn cultivates courage, compassion and contentment in every day life. This tradition is introduced through meditation instruction and explored further through courses, retreats and 'open house' evenings, which offer a meditation practice followed by an insightful talk by one of Shambhala's senior meditation teachers.

The centre has a main shrine room beautifully decorated with traditional meditation aids, Buddhist and Tibetan icons and well stocked with comfy meditation cushions. There's also an adjoining lounge area and other smaller rooms that are used for personal practice and the complimentary meditation interviews offered by the faculty of Shambhala teaching staff.

Ms CUPCAKE

408 Coldharbour Lane, Brixton SW9 8LF
Tel: 020 7733 9438

Online	www.mscupcake.co.uk
	@misscupcakeuk
Hours	Mon-Tues: 11am-6pm
	Weds-Sat: 11am-7pm
	Sun: 11am-5pm
Average price	£2.50 for a cupcake
Tubes	Brixton
Buses	2, 3, P4, 59, 196, 322, 432 - Brixton Tube

WELLBEING EAT

London's first entirely vegan bakery was founded by Melissa Morgan, a gregarious ex-primary school teacher and Brixton local, who's made it her mission to ensure vegans will never be deprived of one of life's greatest pleasures. Although made with vegan ingredients, Melissa claims that her cupcakes, cookies, tray bakes and brownies are the "naughtiest cakes in town" - purposefully indulgent and decadent. Not that anyone seems deterred by the lack of healthy credentials. Ms Cupcake has grown from Melissa's home kitchen, to a Greenwich market stall, to the Brixton shop in less than a year – and there's a cookery book and TV series in the pipeline for 2013.

Inside, the vintage décor and the staff's retro 1950's headscarves place Ms Cupcake back in an era when baking was effortlessly cool and kitsch, world's apart from the industry bandwagon it has become over the past few years. And outside, in typical Brixton community spirit, Ms Cupcake shares outdoor seating with the hugely popular Rosie's Deli - so customers can wash down their cake with a cuppa from Rosie next door.

WAGFREE CAFÉ

26 Brixton Market, Brixton SW9 8PR
Tel: 020 7274 6267

Online	www.wagfreefood.com @wagfree
Hours	Mon-Fri: 10am-8pm Sat: 9am-6pm Sun: 10am-5pm
Average price	£2.70 for a pie / piece of cake
Tubes	Brixton
Buses	2, 3, P4, 59, 196, 322, 432 - Brixton Tube

WELLBEING EAT

When native Northerner, David was diagnosed with coeliac disease, he was bereft at no longer being able to enjoy his diet of beloved beer, bread, pie and chips. Unimpressed with the gluten free ranges of food on offer, which he deemed crumbly and tasteless, David began to experiment with gluten free ingredients and despite no formal previous kitchen experience, succeeded in creating gluten-free versions of his favourite foods he'd so dearly missed - beer battered chips and steak pies included.

With the help of his business partner, wheat-eating Edward Barrow, WAGfree (wheat and gluten free) Café was born and set up shop in the heart of Brixton's recently renovated 1930's undercover market, where it fits in nicely with the diverse blend of artisan and antiquated traders populating the bustling space.

Fish and chips, rustic loaves, smoked quiches, chocolate brownies and treacle tarts are just a handful of the gluten-free fare on the menu, which caters for customers wanting an evening meal (thus making the most of the 10pm closing hours), or for those who simply want to pop in for a snack. The signature WAGon wheel treat – a divine concoction of two almond biscuits sandwiching marshmallow and covered in Montezuma's chocolate – is highly recommended and best enjoyed alongside a cup of WAG's own blend of tea or coffee.

With all produce baked in a dedicated gluten-free bakery WAGfree pride themselves on guaranteeing customers a worry-free experience, where they can eat anything on the menu without a further thought. In addition to the menu, WAGfree also sell specially selected wheat and gluten-free products from other makers, including DIALSI pasta from Italy and Glebe Farm gluten-free oats, granola and muesli. David has also recently added some dairy-free options to the menu for their lactose intolerant coeliac customers.

Occupying a corner stall in Brixton market, WAGfree is slightly limited on space but has enough undercover seating for about 15 covers, and a steady stream of take-away customers, many of whom make daily or weekly pilgrimages to take home their gluten-free fix. Unconcerned with ostentatious décor, WAGfree let's the food speak for itself.

If excellent quality, gluten-free food is WAGfree's primary concern, their contribution to Brixton comes a close second. Although born in Manchester (and still with an accent thick enough to lend proper authenticity to the steak, pie and chips on the menu), David and Edward have lived in Brixton for 40 years and work hard to drive profit and jobs back into their adopted hometown by employing local apprentices and participants in government job-finding schemes, whilst working 14 hour days, 7 days a week to serve their beloved Brixton.

TOOTING BEC LIDO

Tooting Bec Road SW16 1RU
Tel: 020 8871 7198

Online	www.dcleisurecentres.co.uk/centres/tooting-bec-lido/ @ slsclido
Hours	19th May-31st Aug: Mon-Sun: 6am-7pm 1st-30th Sept: Mon-Sun: 6am-4.30pm
Average price	Adults £6, Children & OAPs £3.70
Tubes	Tooting Bec / Streatham
Buses	249, 319 - Tooting Bec Lido, G1 - Garrad's Road

WELLBEING · MOVE

A s well as being the largest swimming pool by surface area in the UK (measuring a lengthy 100 yards and 33 yards wide), Tooting Bec Lido is also one of Britain's oldest open air pools, open to the public since July 1906.

Set on Tooting Bec Common amongst trees and birdsong, the lido's fetching red, yellow and green changing cubicles line the poolside and there's a café serving drinks and snacks to revive yourself after an invigorating dip. Management of the lido is shared between Wandsworth Council, who open the lido to members of the public from late May to late September, and the South London Swimming Club who have exclusive access to the pool throughout the rest of the year – a set up that saved the lido from closure due to financial cut-backs in 1990.

In a city where new ventures and venues are opening every week, it's pleasing to see how Tooting Bec Lido has become such an asset to the local community whilst remaining an iconic 107 year old local hero.

LISTINGS
OTHER SOUTH LONDON WELLBEING DESTINATIONS

THE WHOLEMEAL CAFÉ
1 Shrubbery Road SW16 2AS
www.wholemealcafe.com
Hours: Mon-Sun: 12pm-10pm
Trains: Streatham Rail
Buses: 50, 118, 249, 250, 315 - St Leonard's Church

COOPERS NATURAL FOODS
17 Lower Marsh SE1 7RJ
www.coopersnaturalfoods.com
Hours: Mon-Fri: 8am-5.30pm, Sat: 10am-3.30pm
Trains: Waterloo Rail & Tube / Lambeth North Tube
Buses: 12, 53, 76, 148, 159, 453 - Lower Marsh

BONNINGTON CAFÉ
11 Vauxhall Grove SW8 1TD
www.bonningtoncafe.co.uk
Hours: Mon-Sun: 12-3pm & 6.30-10.30pm
Trains: Vauxhall Tube & Rail
Buses: 2, 36, 87, 88, 196, 360 - Vauxhall bus station

VGANGO VEGAN DELICATESSEN

39 Webbs Road, Battersea SW11 6RX
www.vgango.co.uk
Hours: Mon-Tues & Thur-Sat: 7.30am-5pm,
Wed: 7.30am-4pm
Trains: Clapham Junction Rail
Buses: G1, 139 - Salcott Road or 35, 37 - Eccles Road

NATURA CAFE

**First floor, Goldsmiths College Students Union,
New Cross SE14 6NW**
www.naturacafe.co.uk
Hours: Mon-Thurs: 9am-6pm, Fri: 9am-5pm
Trains: New Cross Overground & Rail
Buses: 21, 136, 171, 172, 177, 436- Marquis of
Granby / Goldsmiths

SIVANANDA YOGA VEDANTA CENTRE

51 Felsham Road, Putney SW15 1AZ
www.sivananda.org/london
Hours: Mon-Thurs: 9.45am-9.30pm
Fri: 9.45am-7.30pm, Sat: 10am-3pm, Sun: 3-6pm
Trains: Putney Rail / East Putney Tube
Buses: 14, 74, 85, 93, 424, 485 - Putney Bridge Road

EMBODY WELLNESS

Unit 9, St George Wharf SW8 2LE
www.embodywellness.co.uk
Hours: Mon-Thurs: 7am-9pm, Fri: 8am-9pm
Sat: 8am-5pm, Sun: 9am-2pm
Trains: Vauxhall Rail & Tube
Buses: 2, 36, 87, 88,196, 360 - Vauxhall bus station

THE LITTLE ESCAPE

4 Paxton Mews, Off Westow Street, Crystal Palace SE19 3RW
www.thelittleescape.com
Hours: Mon-Fri: 8am-9pm, Sat & Sun: 10am-6pm
Trains: Crystal Palace Overground / Gypsy Hill Rail
Buses: 249, 322, 417 - Westow Street

THE SHALA ASHTANGA YOGA CENTRE

**Clapham North Arts Centre,
Unit 1R 26-32 Votaire Rd SW4 6DH**
www.theshala.co.uk
Hours: Mon-Thurs: 6.30am-9.30pm, Fri: 6.30am-11am,
Sat: 9am-12pm, Sun: 10-11.30am
Trains: Clapham North Tube/Clapham High Street Rail
Buses: 50, 88, 155 - Clapham North Tube Station

HOT POWER YOGA

Unit 3B, 9 Park Hill SW4 9NS
www.hotpoweryoga.co.uk
Hours: Mon-Fri: 6.30am-9.30pm, Sat: 8am-6.30pm,
Sun: 9.30am-6pm
Trains: Clapham Common Tube
Buses: 35, 37, 137 - Park Hill

FLYING FANTASTIC
AERIAL FITNESS CENTRE

The Wilditch Centre, 48 Culvert Road SW11 5BB
www.flyingfantastic.co.uk
Hours: Mon, Tues & Weds 6.50-9.45pm
Trains: Queenstown Road Rail / Clapham Junction
Buses: 44, 344 - Battersea Park School

TOOTING BEC ATHLETICS TRACK & GYM

Tooting Bec Road SW17 3NP
www.wandsworth.gov.uk
Hours: Mon-Fri: 8am-9pm, Sat & Sun: 8am-7pm
Trains: Tooting Bec / Tooting Broadway Tube
Buses: 155, 219, 355 Hebdon Road

STUDIO 74 PILATES & GYROTONIC STUDIO

Studio 74, 76 Bermondsey Street SE1 3UD
www.studioseventyfour.co.uk/
Hours: Check online for class times.
Trains: London Bridge Rail & Tube
Buses: 47, 343, 381 - Crucifix Lane

BROCKWELL LIDO

Dulwich Road, London SE24 0PA
www.fusion-lifestyle.com/centres/Brockwell_Lido
Hours: Mon-Fri: 6.30am-10pm, Sat: 7.30am-9.30pm
Sun: 7.30am-9pm
Trains: Brixton Tube / Herne Hill Rail
Buses: 3, 37, 196, 690 - Brockwell Lido

SATYANANDA YOGA CENTRE

70 Thurleigh Road, SW12 8UD
www.syclondon.com/
Hours: Mon-Sun. Check online for class times.
Trains: Clapham South
Buses: G1, 319, 690 Rusham Road

WORDS OF WELLBEING

FITNESS

BY
TIM WEEKS

The human body is made up of a series of systems that should all work together in balance and harmony. There is no one simple single solution to attain ultimate wellbeing - what it requires is a long-term view of the bigger picture and a blend of key ingredients. Sounds simple? It is.

Health, fitness, and wellness should be fun and simple. There's no need for fancy equipment which ties you to one particular gym or space. Simply open your eyes and explore your surroundings using the natural environment and thus allowing yourself to exercise anywhere and anytime. This doesn't mean to not engage in fantastic exercise options such as yoga or ballet, but its about not putting all your eggs in one basket and developing a variety of exercise options. It's also important to be able to exercise on your own, as well as with the motivation and encouragement of a group.

Remember that your willingness to exercise is very much determined by your mood, so have strategies in place to motivate you on the days you're struggling. Hurdles such as illness, injury, or 'stuff' (such as family commitments or work pressures) will also inevitably appear, so implement techniques to keep you on that upward curve. But always bear in mind that life is to be enjoyed, so don't over-complicate fitness and wellbeing and turn being healthy into a chore.

So what are these base ingredients for total holistic wellbeing balance?

1. You need to be physically fit. A strong set of heart and lungs.
2. You need to be structurally strong. Every muscle in the body has a role to play

3. You need to eat a good healthy balanced diet. Simple and healthy recipes made with whole foods.

4. You need good quality rest and recovery. Sleep is essential.

5. You need a good state of mind. Happy mind = Happy body.

And the million dollar question: How much do I need to do to achieve 'wellbeing'? That's dependent upon how much time you have. Once you have your time quota, decide on the best options that will result in the best investment of your time – just make sure that all five ingredients above are in the mix.

TIM WEEKS
Tim Weeks London   www.timweeks.co.uk

MEDITATION
BY
JILLIAN LAVENDER

We all live busy lives in the midst of an increasingly fast-paced and hectic world where there is always something to do. Very quickly and often without realising, we get caught in a vortex of doing - but we are not human 'doings', we are human 'beings'. Yet most people have lost access to this fundamental ability to settle down and simply 'be'. Ask yourself this: when was the last time you sat for 20 minutes and did not speak, read, eat, look at a screen, text or write a list?

THE ESSENCE OF MEDITATION

It wasn't always like this. Thousands of years ago the knowledge of how to experience silence alone with activity was well understood. At the core of this ancient knowledge is meditation. The essence of meditation is the ability to step beyond thinking and arrive at the most settled state of awareness – a state of 'being'. In this state our body is resting deeply while the mind is highly alert and balanced.

When we can step beyond thinking and experience simply being, we bring the mind to its least excited state. This is very important for our wellbeing because our body is always a reflection of what is happening in our mind. You are what you think - an anxious, agitated mind creates an anxious, agitated body. A settled mind produces a settled body.

BENEFITS OF MEDITATION

In meditation the mind experiences a state of pure serene inner delight that lies beyond thinking. This delivers a state of deep rest in the physiology - many times deeper than sleep. When our body rests deeply it releases stress and fatigue faster than we accumulate it. This is the key to good mental and physical health. Studies show that a few minutes of meditation morning and early evening delivers many benefits including better sleep, increased energy, lower blood pressure, reduced anxiety and depression, improved physical wellbeing, better memory and concentration and a reversal of the ageing process.

A MINI-TECHNIQUE TO GET YOU STARTED

Learning to meditate is easy but to do it fully and properly requires personal instruction. In the meantime, here is a simple starter tip to give you a taste of what it feels like to experience simply 'being':

A few seconds activating each of your senses is all it takes. Sit comfortably and put your attention on the sounds around you. After 20 seconds begin to notice the smells in the air. Next, take 20 seconds to note the tastes in your mouth. Another 20 seconds on the feel on your skin and end with 20 seconds looking at your immediate environment. In less than two minutes your mind and body are settled and you are back to the present moment - available, calm and connected.

JILLIAN LAVENDER
London Meditation Centre   www.londonmeditationcentre.com

Stretching the City with London yoga classes

Corporate yoga at your office
6 week beginner's courses
Private or shared classes at home
Vinyasa Flow group classes in Angel, N1:
7-8pm on Mondays & Wednesdays

www.stretchingthecity.com

YOGA

BY
SALLY LOVETT

Despite an estimated 30 million people practicing yoga worldwide, aspects of this ancient practice are still met with mysticism and bewilderment – a dilemma which isn't helped by the overwhelming array of types of yoga on offer today. Below is an explanation of some of the styles of yoga you'll typically find on a timetable, as well as a glossary of terms you might hear in class.

TYPES OF YOGA

Derived from the Sanskrit word 'Yuj', meaning to yoke or join, yoga is the union of body, mind and spirit. Many people come to yoga for the physical benefits of increased tone, flexibility and strength, but are often pleasantly surprised to find themselves feeling mentally more alert, emotionally more stable and more present in their daily life. A typical class will entail yoga postures (asanas), pranayama (breath work) and meditation. Whilst all types of yoga conform to this overarching definition, different schools and styles of yoga differ in their approach and delivery.

Ashtanga yoga is a series of sequenced postures synchronised with the breath. A physically demanding practice, it's best to have mastered the basic yoga postures with hatha classes before moving on to Ashtanga.

Bikram yoga is a series of 26 postures performed in a room heated to 40°c – enabling the loosening of tight muscles and a great deal of detoxifying sweating. Also forms the basis of other 'Hot yoga' styles.

Hatha yoga is the general term used for yoga in the West and it's slower-paced classes and integration of the basic yoga poses make it a great class for beginners.

Iyengar yoga is based on the teachings of BKS Iyengar and places an emphasis on body alignment, using yoga props such as blocks, blankets and belts to aid precise alignment in postures.

Restorative yoga is a deeply relaxing style that promotes deep rest, renewal and restoration through supported passive postures.

Vinyasa yoga (also know as 'flow') links movement with breath to flow through sequences of yoga postures. Sequences vary with each class, so expect more variety than an Ashtanga class.

YOGA GLOSSARY

Chakra – A wheel that radiates life force energy (or prana) around the body. Traditionally, there are seven chakras located from the base of the spine to the crown of head, each correlating to different functions, features, colours and sounds.

Namaste – Meaning 'the light in me honours the light in you', Namaste is a salutation typically said by the teacher, and then repeated by the student(s) at the end of the class.

Om is a single-sound mantra, sound and vibration that represents the unification of the body, mind, spirit and connection of 'oneness' with the universe. Often chanted at the beginning and end of class.

Pranayama is control of the breath and consists of breathing exercises and techniques which regulate the prana (vital life force) within the body.

Savasana, also known as 'corpse pose', is the well-earned rest, relaxation and meditation at the end of the class.

SALLY LOVETT
Stretching The City   www.stretchingthecity.com

Going bananas on deciding what to wear for class?

Experienced yoga instructor *Mollie McClelland* (www.molliemcclelland.com) enlightens us with ten tips when choosing yoga-friendly clothes, which will keep you comfortable, confident and poised in practice.

• Move around in clothing when you try it on, ensure the neckline is appropriate when you bend backwards and your sides don't roll up when you move.

• Choose clothes made of comfortable fabrics. Be aware you might get hot in a class, so sometimes natural fabrics feel better than synthetic in high temperatures, specially bamboo or banana, which soak up and release moisture quickly, so clothes feel less heavy.

• Clothing should fit well: not too tight or loose. It should cover what it needs to without constant adjustments - leaving you free to focus on your breath.

• For poses like downward facing dog and inverted positions, clothing should stay close to your body and not falling on face.

• Check that your clothing, especially the bottoms, are not see through!

• Choose tops that are supportive, but not too tight. Prana circulates within the body and on the skin, so breathability is equally important.

• Layers can be really helpful if you get warmer and then cooler during the course of a session.

• Avoid clothes that have hard objects like buckles and zips attached to them.

• Wear clothes you feel great in!

Mollie's choice:
Carrot, Banana & Peach offers authentic, eco-friendly and sustainable yoga wear. These pioneers of bamboo, organic cotton and beechwood now offer banana and aloe vera to their stylish and beautiful products. Discover how the inherent properties of plants and fruits can enhance your class or practice at: **www.carrotbananapeach.com**

Wellbeing beyond London

Although this book is a celebration of London's healthiest hot spots and wellbeing wonders, there's no denying that sometimes we need a break from the city altogether.

For the ultimate immersion in wellbeing, AdventureYogi run holidays and retreats, where twice daily yoga classes, delicious vegetarian meals, indulgent treatments and optional adventurous activities promise to relax and refresh body, mind and spirit - leaving you suitably rejuvenated and raring to go on your return to the big smoke. Set in stunning venues throughout the UK and Europe, AdventureYogi holidays combine skiing, surfing, hiking or diving with yoga and treatments, whilst their retreats take a slightly slower pace, and free time can be spent curled up with a book, exploring the gorgeous surrounds or having an indulgent afternoon nap.

If you're tempted to treat yourself in 2013, here's a few highlights from the AdventureYogi schedule, with plenty more to be found online:

January: WellbeingYogi, Somerset

February: DetoxYogi, Sussex

March: SnowYogi, France

April: SurfYogi, Cornwall

May: BeachYogi, Ibiza

www.adventureyogi.com

Adventure Yogi   active relaxation

NUTRITION

BY
AMELIA FREER

> **"W**e are indeed much more than what we eat, but what we eat can nevertheless help us to be much more than what we are"
>
> **Adelle Davis**

THE ROLE OF FOOD

Hippocrates told us to use food as our medicine hundreds of years ago, but somewhere along the way our demand for variety and convenience has clouded our respect for the primal role that food plays in wellbeing. Our relationship with food has become complex and emotional and for many in the UK and elsewhere in the developed world, eating has become a leisure pursuit and cooking a hobby. Yet our bodies are still hard-wired for a tougher world where food means survival. Our environment & food sources have evolved in a way that is virtually unrecognizable to our bodies. At what cost to our health? Are our bodies able to adapt, accommodate and survive, healthy and well with the way we feed ourselves in 2013?

In 2001 The World Health Organisation (WHO) stated "More than one billion adults worldwide are overweight, and at least 300 million of these are clinically obese. Up to 80% of cases of coronary heart disease, 90% of type 2 diabetes cases, and one-third of cancers can be avoided by changing to a healthier diet, increasing physical activity and stopping smoking."

WHAT IS NUTRITIONAL THERAPY?

Nutritional Therapy employs an individual-centred approach to healthcare, helping clients to optimise their diet to support and maintain a state of optimal health through the use of specific foods, food concentrates, biological agents and lifestyle changes. Seeking the advice of a nutritional therapist can guide, support and encourage an individual through their journey towards optimal wellbeing.

Being conscious about what, when and how, we consume has a direct impact on wellbeing. But poor food choices and habits are becoming more and more common due to confusing messages from the food and diet industries and our ever-demanding lifestyles.

GETTING STARTED

Eating food in its natural form is always my principle message. This doesn't have to remove the enjoyment of food but it does mean cooking from scratch, with fresh ingredients. The gathering of companions to share and enjoy food is an enriching, essential part of wellbeing and something I always encourage. Taking time to eat, to chew properly can help to control portion sizes and reduce cravings later in the day. And eating in a relaxed environment, not while on the phone, at your desk or in your car, can reduce dependency on convenience foods and support your natural digestive process. A varied and colorful diet will provide a full spectrum of nutrients so think of a rainbow when planning your meals each day and check that you are getting in red, purple, green and yellow instead of only beige foods. Healthy eating isn't so convenient nowadays and so planning ahead ensures better habits. And don't assume that fast food has to be made up of words you can't pronounce - fresh fruit, nuts and seeds are just as fast.

Being conscious about when you choose to eat, taking time for your meals and learning what and how to cook, using fresh ingredients, can really make it possible to eat for both pleasure and health.

AMELIA FREER   www.freernutrition.com

HOLISTIC THERAPIES

BY
LILJA KATANKA

Holistic (or 'Complimentary') therapies treat the client as a whole, taking into account all aspects of the client's physiological, psychological and emotional needs. Firmly believing that stress and emotions can have a direct effect on our health, holistic therapies aim to re-balance the body energetically and are also commonly used preventatively to help support overall good health.

Unlike prescriptive Western medicine, holistic therapies are tailored to the client's needs and place an emphasis on treating the cause as well as the symptoms. It's important to always choose a holistic therapist who is qualified and adequately accredited. To help you choose a treatment, here's an explanation of some popular types of holistic therapy.

Acupuncture is a practice that uses very fine needles to regulate the energy of the body. Evolved over thousands of years from China, acupuncture is commonly used to treat pain, but as a holistic therapy it is also widely used for everything from fertility to fatigue, from reflux to relaxation.

Cranio-Sacral Therapy is a gentle-touch therapy that recognises that the fluids of the body move with a rhythm, and changes to this rhythm can be signs of blockages or ill-health. Therapists use gentle adjustments to help regulate these rhythms and the flow of energy. The practice has become most well-known for treating new-born babies and mothers after the impact of birth, but can be used for a wide variety of physical and emotional issues.

Energy Healing such as **Reiki** is channelled through the practitioner's hands to the client. This energy is known as 'life-force' energy and is encouraged to flow within our bodies, promoting healing and a sense of wellbeing.

Homeopathy is a safe, non-toxic form of treatment that can have surprisingly powerful effects. Treatment is based on the principle of 'like-treats-like': in the same way as immunisations may use a tiny amount of a pathogen to stimulate the body's immune response, homeopathic remedies may contain a miniscule amount of a herb or substance which, in higher doses, could cause the symptoms being treated.

MASSAGE THERAPIES

There are countless styles of massage therapies available, and each practitioner may have developed their own style. Holistic and Swedish massage may include some deep tissue techniques if appropriate, and practitioners might incorporate elements of acupressure or stretches into their treatment. Massage has consistently been shown to help relieve stress, benefit the immune system and circulation, and improve lymph drainage. It can also benefit muscles and joints, treat specific pain, emotional issues and improve digestion.

Aromatherapy massage uses specific essential oils tailored to the individual. Essential oils are derived from plants and can have powerful healing properties through their scents, which soothe the skin, body and in some cases, mind.

Thai Yoga Massage and **Shiatsu** are specific types of bodywork that originated from Thailand and Japan respectively. Both work on energy channels or meridians, and are performed through clothing, usually on a mat on the floor. Shiatsu can be used for more specific ailments as well as relaxation and flexibility, whereas Thai Yoga Massage has more emphasis on passive stretches and deep pressure.

Reflexology is based on the principle that the feet reflect a map of the body, so by working with a gentle pressure on the feet to access corresponding places in the body it is possible to treat many conditions and restore natural balance.

Treat yourself to a holistic therapy at home... If you have trouble sleeping, massage the soles of your feet before bed, either 'dry' or with oil (a drop or two of diluted lavender oil or warm sesame oil can be lovely) until they are warm and tingly. Focus on the point about a third of the way from the toes to the heel. As well as making your feet nice and warm, this helps to draws the excess energy down from the head and over-active mind, and lets you nod off peacefully.

LILJA KATANKA
The Little Escape   www.thelittleescape.com

WELLBEING WORLDWIDE

WHEN LONDON FAILS TO DELIVER SUNNY SKIES AND WARM CLIMES, LOOK NO FURTHER THAN THESE FOUR EXOTIC RETREATS FOR THE ULTIMATE WELLBEING HOLIDAY.

FIVELEMENTS, BALI

Based on the banks of Bali's sacred Ayung River, this holistic healing centre is founded on Balinese traditions of health and wellbeing. The perfect place to nurture, nourish and recharge.

www.fivelements.org

BARBERYN AYURVEDA RESORTS, SRI LANKA

Choose from two resorts in Sri Lanka, both of which combine the indulgence of a luxury beach holiday with the healing powers of professional Ayurvedic treatments, meals, yoga and meditation.

www.barberynresorts.com

1711 TI SANA DETOX RETREAT, ITALY

Set amongst the lakes and mountains of Italy's Adda valley, Ti Sana offers ancient rituals of purification and contemporary body and beauty treatments for the ultimate indulgent detox experience.

www.1711.it

ASHIYANA YOGA AND SPA VILLAGE, INDIA

Meaning 'home' in Hindi, Ashiyana is set on the beaches of North Goa amidst abundant tropical flora and fauna, and offers yoga retreats and trainings, rejuvenating spa breaks and revitalising detox packages.

www.ashiyana-yoga-goa.com

FINDING PEACE, SERENITY AND SOLACE OVERSEAS

THANKS

For your love, support, inspiration and encouragement: Jean and Andrew Lovett, Katy and Scott Chambers, The Monsters (aka Oliver and Sophia), The Uglows, Jenny Allen-Smith and her beautiful brood, Oliver Moran, The Park Village posse and the Perkins pals, the Lormand-Payne/Georgiou ladies: Sophia, Tanya, Juliana, Aimee, Diane and Sylvie, and the Stretching the City yoga students who turn up on their mats week in, week out.

Also big thanks to the following people for making this book happen: Alex Evans at Vespertine Press, Matt Baker and James Kirkup for their stellar design work, Ali Gunning, Ariadna Bakhmatova, Julie Robinson, Tessa Watt, Tim Weeks, Amelia Freer, Jillian Lavender, Lilja Katanka, AdventureYogi's Michelle King and Claire Hamilton, Paul and the team at Yogamatters.

And to all the people behind the wonderful wellbeing places we visited over the summer of 2012, who shared their stories with us, fed, spoilt and indulged us, and made us feel so very welcome.

GET IN TOUCH

www.wellbeing-london.com
hello@wellbeing-london.com
@Wellbeing_LDN